Connected Mathematics 2

# Filling and Wrapping

## Three-Dimensional Measurement

**Glenda Lappan**

**James T. Fey**

**William M. Fitzgerald**

**Susan N. Friel**

**Elizabeth Difanis Phillips**

**PEARSON**

Prentice
Hall

Boston, Massachusetts
Upper Saddle River, New Jersey

**Connected Mathematics™ was developed at Michigan State University with financial support from the Michigan State University Office of the Provost, Computing and Technology, and the College of Natural Science.**

 This material is based upon work supported by the National Science Foundation under Grant No. MDR 9150217 and Grant No. ESI 9986372. Opinions expressed are those of the authors and not necessarily those of the Foundation.

The Michigan State University authors and administration have agreed that all MSU royalties arising from this publication will be devoted to purposes supported by the MSU Mathematics Education Enrichment Fund.

**Acknowledgments** appear on page 87, which constitutes an extension of this copyright page.

ISBN 0-13-165644-9

3 4 5 6 7 8 9 10   09 08 07 06

# Authors of Connected Mathematics

*(from left to right)* Glenda Lappan, Betty Phillips, Susan Friel, Bill Fitzgerald, Jim Fey

**Glenda Lappan** is a University Distinguished Professor in the Department of Mathematics at Michigan State University. Her research and development interests are in the connected areas of students' learning of mathematics and mathematics teachers' professional growth and change related to the development and enactment of K–12 curriculum materials.

**James T. Fey** is a Professor of Curriculum and Instruction and Mathematics at the University of Maryland. His consistent professional interest has been development and research focused on curriculum materials that engage middle and high school students in problem-based collaborative investigations of mathematical ideas and their applications.

**William M. Fitzgerald** *(Deceased)* was a Professor in the Department of Mathematics at Michigan State University. His early research was on the use of concrete materials in supporting student learning and led to the development of teaching materials for laboratory environments. Later he helped develop a teaching model to support student experimentation with mathematics.

**Susan N. Friel** is a Professor of Mathematics Education in the School of Education at the University of North Carolina at Chapel Hill. Her research interests focus on statistics education for middle-grade students and, more broadly, on teachers' professional development and growth in teaching mathematics K–8.

**Elizabeth Difanis Phillips** is a Senior Academic Specialist in the Mathematics Department of Michigan State University. She is interested in teaching and learning mathematics for both teachers and students. These interests have led to curriculum and professional development projects at the middle school and high school levels, as well as projects related to the teaching and learning of algebra across the grades.

# CMP2 Development Staff

# Field Test Sites for CMP2

**D**uring the development of the revised edition of *Connected Mathematics* (CMP2), more than 100 classroom teachers have field-tested materials at 49 school sites in 12 states and the District of Columbia. This classroom testing occurred over three academic years (2001 through 2004), allowing careful study of the effectiveness of each of the 24 units that comprise the program. A special thanks to the students and teachers at these pilot schools.

## Arkansas
**Magnolia Public Schools**
Kittena Bell*, Judith Trowell*; *Central Elementary School:* Maxine Broom, Betty Eddy, Tiffany Fallin, Bonnie Flurry, Carolyn Monk, Elizabeth Tye; *Magnolia Junior High School:* Monique Bryan, Ginger Cook, David Graham, Shelby Lamkin

## Colorado
**Boulder Public Schools**
*Nevin Platt Middle School:* Judith Koenig

**St. Vrain Valley School District, Longmont**
*Westview Middle School:* Colleen Beyer, Kitty Canupp, Ellie Decker*, Peggy McCarthy, Tanya deNobrega, Cindy Payne, Ericka Pilon, Andrew Roberts

## District of Columbia
*Capitol Hill Day School:* Ann Lawrence

## Georgia
**University of Georgia, Athens**
Brad Findell

**Madison Public Schools**
*Morgan County Middle School:* Renee Burgdorf, Lynn Harris, Nancy Kurtz, Carolyn Stewart

## Maine
**Falmouth Public Schools**
*Falmouth Middle School:* Donna Erikson, Joyce Hebert, Paula Hodgkins, Rick Hogan, David Legere, Cynthia Martin, Barbara Stiles, Shawn Towle*

* indicates a Field Test Site Coordinator

## Michigan
**Portland Public Schools**
*Portland Middle School:* Mark Braun, Holly DeRosia, Kathy Dole*, Angie Foote, Teri Keusch, Tammi Wardwell

**Traverse City Area Public Schools**
*Bertha Vos Elementary:* Kristin Sak; *Central Grade School:* Michelle Clark; Jody Meyers; *Eastern Elementary:* Karrie Tufts; *Interlochen Elementary:* Mary McGee-Cullen; *Long Lake Elementary:* Julie Faulkner*, Charlie Maxbauer, Katherine Sleder; *Norris Elementary:* Hope Slanaker; *Oak Park Elementary:* Jessica Steed; *Traverse Heights Elementary:* Jennifer Wolfert; *Westwoods Elementary:* Nancy Conn; *Old Mission Peninsula School:* Deb Larimer; *Traverse City East Junior High:* Ivanka Berkshire, Ruthanne Kladder, Jan Palkowski, Jane Peterson, Mary Beth Schmitt; *Traverse City West Junior High:* Dan Fouch*, Ray Fouch

**Sturgis Public Schools**
*Sturgis Middle School:* Ellen Eisele

## Minnesota
**Burnsville School District 191**
*Hidden Valley Elementary:* Stephanie Cin, Jane McDevitt

**Hopkins School District 270**
*Alice Smith Elementary:* Sandra Cowing, Kathleen Gustafson, Martha Mason, Scott Stillman; *Eisenhower Elementary:* Chad Bellig, Patrick Berger, Nancy Glades, Kye Johnson, Shane Wasserman, Victoria Wilson; *Gatewood Elementary:* Sarah Ham, Julie Kloos, Janine Pung, Larry Wade; *Glen Lake Elementary:* Jacqueline Cramer, Kathy Hering, Cecelia Morris,

Robb Trenda; *Katherine Curren Elementary:* Diane Bancroft, Sue DeWit, John Wilson; *L. H. Tanglen Elementary:* Kevin Athmann, Lisa Becker, Mary LaBelle, Kathy Rezac, Roberta Severson; *Meadowbrook Elementary:* Jan Gauger, Hildy Shank, Jessica Zimmerman; *North Junior High:* Laurel Hahn, Kristin Lee, Jodi Markuson, Bruce Mestemacher, Laurel Miller, Bonnie Rinker, Jeannine Salzer, Sarah Shafer, Cam Stottler; *West Junior High:* Alicia Beebe, Kristie Earl, Nobu Fujii, Pam Georgetti, Susan Gilbert, Regina Nelson Johnson, Debra Lindstrom, Michele Luke*, Jon Sorenson

**Minneapolis School District 1**
*Ann Sullivan K-8 School:* Bronwyn Collins; Anne Bartel* (Curriculum and Instruction Office)

**Wayzata School District 284**
*Central Middle School:* Sarajane Myers, Dan Nielsen, Tanya Ravenholdt

**White Bear Lake School District 624**
*Central Middle School:* Amy Jorgenson, Michelle Reich, Brenda Sammon

## New York
**New York City Public Schools**
*IS 89:* Yelena Aynbinder, Chi-Man Ng, Nina Rapaport, Joel Spengler, Phyllis Tam*, Brent Wyso; *Wagner Middle School:* Jason Appel, Intissar Fernandez, Yee Gee Get, Richard Goldstein, Irving Marcus, Sue Norton, Bernadita Owens, Jennifer Rehn*, Kevin Yuhas

### Ohio

**Talawanda School District, Oxford**
*Talawanda Middle School:* Teresa Abrams, Larry Brock, Heather Brosey, Julie Churchman, Monna Even, Karen Fitch, Bob George, Amanda Klee, Pat Meade, Sandy Montgomery, Barbara Sherman, Lauren Steidl

**Miami University**
Jeffrey Wanko*

**Springfield Public Schools**
*Rockway School:* Jim Mamer

### Pennsylvania

**Pittsburgh Public Schools**
Kenneth Labuskes, Marianne O'Connor, Mary Lynn Raith*; *Arthur J. Rooney Middle School:* David Hairston, Stamatina Mousetis, Alfredo Zangaro; *Frick International Studies Academy:* Suzanne Berry, Janet Falkowski, Constance Finseth, Romika Hodge, Frank Machi; *Reizenstein Middle School:* Jeff Baldwin, James Brautigam, Lorena Burnett, Glen Cobbett, Michael Jordan, Margaret Lazur, Melissa Munnell, Holly Neely, Ingrid Reed, Dennis Reft

### Texas

**Austin Independent School District**
*Bedichek Middle School:* Lisa Brown, Jennifer Glasscock, Vicki Massey

**El Paso Independent School District**
*Cordova Middle School:* Armando Aguirre, Anneliesa Durkes, Sylvia Guzman, Pat Holguin*, William Holguin, Nancy Nava, Laura Orozco, Michelle Peña, Roberta Rosen, Patsy Smith, Jeremy Wolf

**Plano Independent School District**
Patt Henry, James Wohlgehagen*; *Frankford Middle School:* Mandy Baker, Cheryl Butsch, Amy Dudley, Betsy Eshelman, Janet Greene, Cort Haynes, Kathy Letchworth, Kay Marshall, Kelly McCants, Amy Reck, Judy Scott, Syndy Snyder, Lisa Wang; *Wilson Middle School:* Darcie Bane, Amanda Bedenko, Whitney Evans, Tonelli Hatley, Sarah (Becky) Higgs, Kelly Johnston, Rebecca McElligott, Kay Neuse, Cheri Slocum, Kelli Straight

### Washington

**Evergreen School District**
*Shahala Middle School:* Nicole Abrahamsen, Terry Coon*, Carey Doyle, Sheryl Drechsler, George Gemma, Gina Helland, Amy Hilario, Darla Lidyard, Sean McCarthy, Tilly Meyer, Willow Neuwelt, Todd Parsons, Brian Pederson, Stan Posey, Shawn Scott, Craig Sjoberg, Lynette Sundstrom, Charles Switzer, Luke Youngblood

### Wisconsin

**Beaver Dam Unified School District**
*Beaver Dam Middle School:* Jim Braemer, Jeanne Frick, Jessica Greatens, Barbara Link, Dennis McCormick, Karen Michels, Nancy Nichols*, Nancy Palm, Shelly Stelsel, Susan Wiggins

* indicates a Field Test Site Coordinator

# Reviews of CMP to Guide Development of CMP2

**B**efore writing for CMP2 began or field tests were conducted, the first edition of *Connected Mathematics* was submitted to the mathematics faculties of school districts from many parts of the country and to 80 individual reviewers for extensive comments.

## School District Survey Reviews of CMP

**Arizona**
Madison School District #38 (Phoenix)

**Arkansas**
Cabot School District, Little Rock School District, Magnolia School District

**California**
Los Angeles Unified School District

**Colorado**
St. Vrain Valley School District (Longmont)

**Florida**
Leon County Schools (Tallahassee)

**Illinois**
School District #21 (Wheeling)

**Indiana**
Joseph L. Block Junior High (East Chicago)

**Kentucky**
Fayette County Public Schools (Lexington)

**Maine**
Selection of Schools

**Massachusetts**
Selection of Schools

**Michigan**
Sparta Area Schools

**Minnesota**
Hopkins School District

**Texas**
Austin Independent School District, The El Paso Collaborative for Academic Excellence, Plano Independent School District

**Wisconsin**
Platteville Middle School

# Individual Reviewers of CMP

**Arkansas**
Deborah Cramer; Robby Frizzell *(Taylor)*; Lowell Lynde *(University of Arkansas, Monticello)*; Leigh Manzer *(Norfork)*; Lynne Roberts *(Emerson High School, Emerson)*; Tony Timms *(Cabot Public Schools)*; Judith Trowell *(Arkansas Department of Higher Education)*

**California**
José Alcantar *(Gilroy)*; Eugenie Belcher *(Gilroy)*; Marian Pasternack *(Lowman M. S. T. Center, North Hollywood)*; Susana Pezoa *(San Jose)*; Todd Rabusin *(Hollister)*; Margaret Siegfried *(Ocala Middle School, San Jose)*; Polly Underwood *(Ocala Middle School, San Jose)*

**Colorado**
Janeane Golliher *(St. Vrain Valley School District, Longmont)*; Judith Koenig *(Nevin Platt Middle School, Boulder)*

**Florida**
Paige Loggins *(Swift Creek Middle School, Tallahassee)*

**Illinois**
Jan Robinson *(School District #21, Wheeling)*

**Indiana**
Frances Jackson *(Joseph L. Block Junior High, East Chicago)*

**Kentucky**
Natalee Feese *(Fayette County Public Schools, Lexington)*

**Maine**
Betsy Berry *(Maine Math & Science Alliance, Augusta)*

**Maryland**
Joseph Gagnon *(University of Maryland, College Park)*; Paula Maccini *(University of Maryland, College Park)*

**Massachusetts**
George Cobb *(Mt. Holyoke College, South Hadley)*; Cliff Kanold *(University of Massachusetts, Amherst)*

**Michigan**
Mary Bouck *(Farwell Area Schools)*; Carol Dorer *(Slauson Middle School, Ann Arbor)*; Carrie Heaney *(Forsythe Middle School, Ann Arbor)*; Ellen Hopkins *(Clague Middle School, Ann Arbor)*; Teri Keusch *(Portland Middle School, Portland)*; Valerie Mills *(Oakland Schools, Waterford)*; Mary Beth Schmitt *(Traverse City East Junior High, Traverse City)*; Jack Smith *(Michigan State University, East Lansing)*; Rebecca Spencer *(Sparta Middle School, Sparta)*; Ann Marie Nicoll Turner *(Tappan Middle School, Ann Arbor)*; Scott Turner *(Scarlett Middle School, Ann Arbor)*

**Minnesota**
Margarita Alvarez *(Olson Middle School, Minneapolis)*; Jane Amundson *(Nicollet Junior High, Burnsville)*; Anne Bartel *(Minneapolis Public Schools)*; Gwen Ranzau Campbell *(Sunrise Park Middle School, White Bear Lake)*; Stephanie Cin *(Hidden Valley Elementary, Burnsville)*; Joan Garfield *(University of Minnesota, Minneapolis)*; Gretchen Hall *(Richfield Middle School, Richfield)*; Jennifer Larson *(Olson Middle School, Minneapolis)*; Michele Luke *(West Junior High, Minnetonka)*; Jeni Meyer *(Richfield Junior High, Richfield)*; Judy Pfingsten *(Inver Grove Heights Middle School, Inver Grove Heights)*; Sarah Shafer *(North Junior High, Minnetonka)*; Genni Steele *(Central Middle School, White Bear Lake)*; Victoria Wilson *(Eisenhower Elementary, Hopkins)*; Paul Zorn *(St. Olaf College, Northfield)*

**New York**
Debra Altenau-Bartolino *(Greenwich Village Middle School, New York)*; Doug Clements *(University of Buffalo)*; Francis Curcio *(New York University, New York)*; Christine Dorosh *(Clinton School for Writers, Brooklyn)*; Jennifer Rehn *(East Side Middle School, New York)*; Phyllis Tam *(IS 89 Lab School, New York)*;

Marie Turini *(Louis Armstrong Middle School, New York)*; Lucy West *(Community School District 2, New York)*; Monica Witt *(Simon Baruch Intermediate School 104, New York)*

**Pennsylvania**
Robert Aglietti *(Pittsburgh)*; Sharon Mihalich *(Pittsburgh)*; Jennifer Plumb *(South Hills Middle School, Pittsburgh)*; Mary Lynn Raith *(Pittsburgh Public Schools)*

**Texas**
Michelle Bittick *(Austin Independent School District)*; Margaret Cregg *(Plano Independent School District)*; Sheila Cunningham *(Klein Independent School District)*; Judy Hill *(Austin Independent School District)*; Patricia Holguin *(El Paso Independent School District)*; Bonnie McNemar *(Arlington)*; Kay Neuse *(Plano Independent School District)*; Joyce Polanco *(Austin Independent School District)*; Marge Ramirez *(University of Texas at El Paso)*; Pat Rossman *(Baker Campus, Austin)*; Cindy Schimek *(Houston)*; Cynthia Schneider *(Charles A. Dana Center, University of Texas at Austin)*; Uri Treisman *(Charles A. Dana Center, University of Texas at Austin)*; Jacqueline Weilmuenster *(Grapevine-Colleyville Independent School District)*; LuAnn Weynand *(San Antonio)*; Carmen Whitman *(Austin Independent School District)*; James Wohlgehagen *(Plano Independent School District)*

**Washington**
Ramesh Gangolli *(University of Washington, Seattle)*

**Wisconsin**
Susan Lamon *(Marquette University, Hales Corner)*; Steve Reinhart *(retired, Chippewa Falls Middle School, Eau Claire)*

# Table of Contents

# Filling and Wrapping
## Three-Dimensional Measurement

# Filling and Wrapping

## Three-Dimensional Measurement

**B**aseballs, basketballs, and soccer balls are spheres, but they often come in boxes shaped liked cubes. Why do you think balls are packaged in this way?

**A** popcorn vendor needs to order popcorn boxes. A rectangular box has a height of 20 centimeters and a square base with 12-centimeter sides. A cylindrical box has a height of 20 centimeters and a diameter of 12 centimeters. Which box will hold the most popcorn?

**A** rectangular compost box with dimensions 1 foot by 2 feet by 3 feet can decompose 0.5 pounds of garbage a day. Describe the dimensions of a box that will decompose 1 pound of garbage a day.

The way a product is packaged is important. Stores are filled with interesting three-dimensional shapes such as boxes, cans, bags, and bottles. A unique shape can attract shoppers to take a closer look at the product. When a company plans the packaging for a product, it must consider several questions, including how much of the product should be sold in each package; what and how much material is needed to make the package; and what package design is best for the product.

Thinking about how products are packaged can make you a smarter consumer. You can usually save money by comparing the cost of products in different-sized packages.

In this unit, you will look at two different measures involved in three-dimensional shapes. You will explore how much material it takes to *fill* a shape and how much material is needed to *wrap* a shape. As you work through the investigations, you will consider questions like those on the opposite page.

# Mathematical Highlights

**I**n *Filling and Wrapping*, you will explore surface area and volume of objects, especially rectangular prisms, cylinders, cones, and spheres.

**You will learn how to**

- Understand volume as a measure of *filling* an object and surface area as a measure of *wrapping* an object

- Develop strategies for finding the volume and surface area of objects including rectangular prisms and cylinders

- Develop strategies for finding the volume of square pyramids, cones, and spheres

- Explore patterns among the volumes of cylinders, cones, and spheres

- Design and use nets for rectangular prisms and cylinders to calculate surface areas of prisms and cylinders

- Understand that three-dimensional figures may have the same volume but different surface areas

- Investigate the effects of varying dimensions of rectangular prisms and cylinders on volume and surface area

- Recognize and solve problems involving volume and surface area

**As you work on problems in this unit, ask yourself questions about volume and surface area.**

*What quantities are involved in the problem? Which measures of an object are involved—volume or surface area?*

*Is an exact answer required?*

*What method should I use to determine these measures?*

*What strategies or formulas might help?*

# Investigation 1

# Building Boxes

The most common type of package is the rectangular box. Rectangular boxes contain everything from cereal to shoes and from pizza to paper clips. Most rectangular boxes begin as flat sheets of cardboard, which are cut and then folded into a box shape.

## 1.1 Making Cubic Boxes

Some boxes are shaped like cubes. A **cube** is a three-dimensional shape with six identical square faces.

*What kinds of things might be packaged in cubic boxes?*

The boxes you will work with in this problem are shaped like unit cubes. A **unit cube** is a cube with edges that are 1 unit long. For example, cubes that are 1 inch on each edge are called inch cubes. Cubes that are 1 centimeter on each edge are called centimeter cubes.

In this problem, you will make nets that can be folded to form boxes. A **net** is a two-dimensional pattern that can be folded to form a three-dimensional figure. The diagram below shows one possible net for a cubic box.

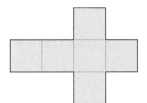 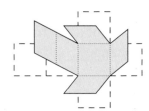

## Problem 1.1 Making Cubic Boxes

On grid paper, draw nets that can be folded to make a unit cube.

**A.** How many different nets can you make that will fold into a box shaped like a unit cube?

**B.** What is the total area of each net, in square units?

ACE Homework starts on page 10.

# 1.2 Making Rectangular Boxes

**M**any boxes are not shaped like cubes. The rectangular box below has square ends, but the remaining faces are non-square rectangles.

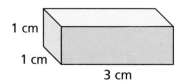

1 cm

1 cm

3 cm

## Problem 1.2 Making Rectangular Boxes

**A.** On grid paper, draw two different nets for the rectangular box above. Cut each pattern out and fold it into a box.

**B.** Describe the faces of the box formed from each net you made. What are the dimensions of each face?

**C.** Find the total area of each net you made in Question A.

**D.** How many centimeter cubes will fit into the box formed from each net you made? Explain your reasoning.

**E.** Suppose you stand the rectangular 1 centimeter × 1 centimeter × 3 centimeters box on its end. Does the area of a net for the box or the number of cubes needed to fill the box change?

ACE Homework starts on page 10.

*active math*
*online*

**For:** Virtual Box Activity
**Visit:** PHSchool.com
**Web Code:** and-6102

**A**ll the boxes you have made so far are rectangular prisms. A **rectangular prism** is a three-dimensional shape with six rectangular faces. The size of a rectangular prism can be described by giving its *dimensions*. The dimensions are the length, the width, and the height.

The **base** of a rectangular prism is the face on the bottom (the face that rests on the table or floor). The length and width of a prism are the length and width of its rectangular base. The height is the distance from the base of the prism to its top.

### Getting Ready for Problem

- Suppose you want to cut the box in the figure below to make a net for the box. Along which edges can you make the cut?

- Are there different choices of edges to cut that will work?

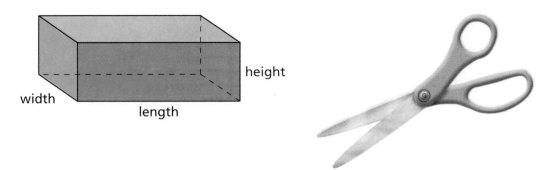

An engineer at the Save-a-Tree packaging company drew the nets below. He lost the notes that indicated the dimensions of the boxes. Use your thinking from the Getting Ready section to work backwards and determine the dimensions for him.

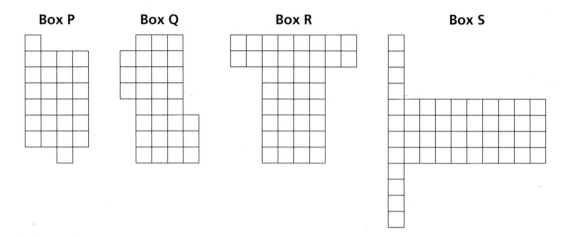

Box P    Box Q    Box R    Box S

## Problem 1.3 Rectangular Prisms

**A.** Using a copy of the diagram above, draw in fold lines and cut each pattern and fold it to form a box. What are the dimensions of each box?

**B.** How are the dimensions of each box related to the dimensions of its faces?

**C.** What is the total area, in square units, of all the faces of each box?

**D.** Fill each box with unit cubes. How many unit cubes does it take to fill each box?

**E.** Design a net for a box that has a different shape than Box P but holds the same number of cubes as Box P.

**ACE** Homework starts on page 10.

## Flattening a Box

**A**my is a packaging engineer at the Save-a-Tree packaging company. Mr. Shu asks Amy to come to his class and explain her job to his students. She gives each student a box to do some exploring.

# Problem 1.4 Surface Area of a Rectangular Prism

Your teacher will give you a box.

**A.** Find the dimensions of the box.

**B.** Use the dimensions of the box to make a net on centimeter grid paper. You may find it helpful to put the box on the paper, outline the base, and then roll the box over so a new face touches the paper.

**C.** Match each face of the box to your net in Question B. Label the net to show how the faces match.

**D.** Amy explained that one thing she considers when designing a box is the cost of the material. Suppose the material for the box costs $\frac{1}{10}$ of a cent per square centimeter. What is the total cost of the material for the box? Why might this information be useful?

**E.** What other information do you think is important to consider when designing a box?

ACE Homework starts on page 10.

## Did You Know?

It is possible to receive a college degree in packaging. A packaging degree prepares a person to develop and produce packages for a variety of products. The designer must pay attention to cost, durability, transportability, safety and environmental regulations, and visual appeal. Many manufacturing companies want people with packaging degrees. However, there are only a few colleges or universities that offer a bachelor's degree in packaging.

 Go Online

PHSchool.com **For:** Information about a degree in packaging **Web Code:** ane-9031

## Applications

**For Exercises 1–4, decide if you can fold the net along the lines to form a closed cubic box. If you are unsure, draw the pattern on grid paper and cut it out to experiment.**

**1.**

**2.**

**3.**

**4.**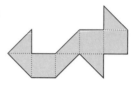

**5.** Which of these nets could be folded along the lines to form a closed rectangular box?

**A.** 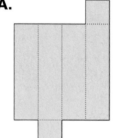　　　**B.** 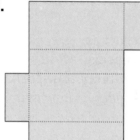　　　**C.**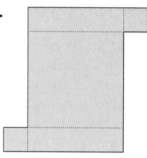

**6.** Do parts (a)–(c) for each pattern from Exercise 5 that forms a closed rectangular box.

   **a.** Use the unit square shown to help you find the dimensions of the box.

   unit square

   **b.** Find the total area, in square units, of all the faces of the box.

   **c.** Find the number of unit cubes it would take to fill the box.

**7.** This closed rectangular box does not have square ends.

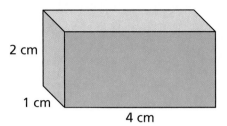

2 cm

1 cm

4 cm

    **a.** What are the dimensions of the box?

    **b.** On centimeter grid paper, sketch two nets for the box.

    **c.** Find the area, in square centimeters, of each net.

    **d.** Find the total area of all the faces of the box. How does your answer compare with the areas you found in part (c)?

**8.** Which of these patterns can be folded along the lines to form a closed rectangular box? Explain.

    **a.**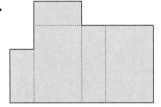

    **b.**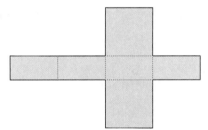

    **c.**

    **d.**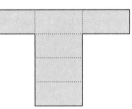

    **e.**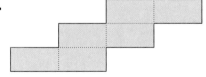

**9.** Can you fold this net along the lines to form an open cubic box? Explain your reasoning.

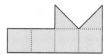

**For each box described in Exercises 10–13:**

- Make a sketch of the box and label the dimensions.
- Draw a net.
- Find the area of each face.
- Find the total area of all the faces.

**10.** a rectangular box with dimensions 2 centimeters × 3 centimeters × 5 centimeters

**11.** a rectangular box with dimensions $2\frac{1}{2}$ centimeters × 2 centimeters × 1 centimeter

**12.** a cubic box with side lengths $3\frac{2}{3}$ centimeters

**13.** a cubic box that holds 125 unit cubes

**14.** An open box is a box without a top.

    **a.** On grid paper, sketch nets for three different open cubic boxes.

    **b.** On grid paper, sketch nets for three different open rectangular boxes (not cubic boxes) with square ends.

    **c.** Find the area of each net you found in parts (a) and (b).

*Homework*
*Help* **O**nline
PHSchool.com

**For:** Help with Exercise 10
**Web Code:** ane-6110

# Connections

For Exercises 15–18, use the following information: A *hexomino* is a shape made of six identical squares connected along their sides. The nets for a closed cubic box are examples of hexominos. Below are five different hexominos.

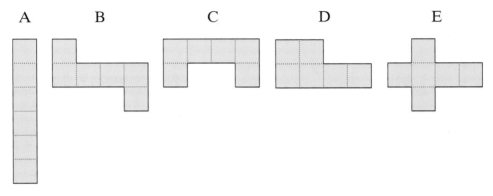

A        B        C        D        E

**15.** Find the perimeter of each hexomino shown above.

**16.** Which hexominos can you fold to form a closed cubic box?

**17.** From which hexominos can you remove one square to make a net for an open cubic box? For each hexomino you select, draw a diagram showing which square can be removed.

**18.** To which hexominos can you add the number of squares below without changing the perimeter? For each hexomino you select, draw a diagram. Explain why the perimeter does not change.

    **a.** one square                     **b.** two squares

**For Exercises 19–22, find the area and the perimeter of each figure. Figures are not drawn to scale.**

**Go Online**
PHSchool.com
**For:** Multiple-Choice Skills
Practice
**Web Code:** ana-6154

**19.**

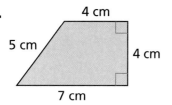

**20.**

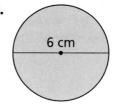

**21.**

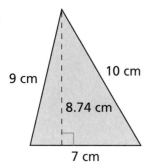

**22.**

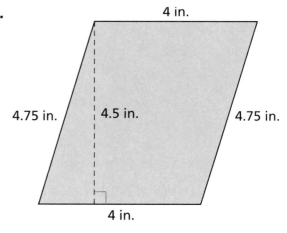

**23.** Which pair of angles are complementary angles?

**a.**

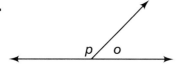

**b.**

**c.**

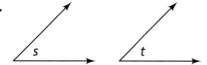

**24.** Angles *m* and *n* below are supplementary angles. Angle *m* has a measure of 78°. What is the measure of angle *n*?

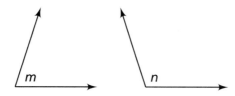

**25. Multiple Choice** Which angle is supplementary to a 57° angle?

A. 123°  B. 57°  C. 33°  D.

**26.** What measurements do you need and how do you use those measurements to find the area and perimeter of each figure below?

   **a.** rectangle   **b.** square

**27.** Mrs. Zhou is making wooden slats for doll beds from a strip of thin board.

She cuts $\frac{1}{12}$ of the strip for another project. Bed slats for one doll bed take $\frac{1}{8}$ of a strip.

$\frac{1}{12}$

   **a.** Suppose Mrs. Zhou uses the remainder of this strip for bed slats. How many doll beds can she make?

   **b.** Draw diagrams to confirm your answer.

**28. a.** Four friends shared $\frac{3}{5}$ of a pizza. What fraction of the pizza did each receive?

**b.** Draw a picture to confirm your answer.

**29.** Mr. Bouck is making snack bars. The recipe calls for $\frac{3}{8}$ stick of butter. He has $3\frac{1}{2}$ sticks on hand.

**a.** How many recipes can he make?

**b.** Draw a picture to show your reasoning.

**30.** Tom plans to plant an herb garden in a glass tank. A scoop of dirt fills 0.15 of the volume of the tank. He needs to put in dirt equal to 65% of the volume. How many scoops of dirt does he need?

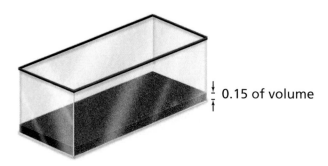

0.15 of volume

**31.** A glass container is 0.5 full of water. After 400 milliliters are poured out, the container is 0.34 full. How much does the container hold?

## Extensions

**32.** A number cube is designed so that numbers on opposite sides add to 7. Write the integers from 1 to 6 on one of the nets you found in Problem 1.1 so that it can be folded to form this number cube. You may want to test your pattern by cutting it out and folding it.

**33.** Examine the nets you made for cubic boxes in Problem 1.1. Suppose you want to make boxes by tracing several copies of the same pattern onto a large sheet of cardboard and cutting them out.

Which pattern allows you to make the greatest number of boxes from a square sheet of cardboard with a side length of 10 units? Test your ideas on grid paper.

# Mathematical Reflections 1

**I**n this investigation, you explored rectangular boxes, and you made nets for boxes. You found the dimensions of a box, the total area of all its faces, and the number of unit cubes required to fill it. These questions will help you summarize what you have learned.

Think about your answers to these questions. Discuss your ideas with other students and your teacher. Then write a summary of your findings in your notebook.

1. Explain how to find the total area of all the faces of a rectangular box.

2. Explain how to find the number of identical cubes it will take to fill a rectangular box.

3. Suppose several different nets are made for a given box. What do all of the nets have in common? What might be different?

# Designing Rectangular Boxes

Finding the right box for a product requires thought and planning. A company must consider how much the box can hold as well as the amount and the cost of the material needed to make the box.

The amount that a box can hold depends on its volume. The **volume** of a box is the number of unit cubes that it would take to fill the box. The amount of material needed to make or to cover a box depends on its surface area. The **surface area** of a box is the total area of all of its faces.

The box shown below has dimensions of 1 centimeter by 3 centimeters by 1 centimeter. It would take three 1-centimeter cubes to fill this box, so the box has a volume of 3 cubic centimeters. Because the net for the box takes fourteen 1-centimeter grid squares to make the box, the box has a surface area of 14 square centimeters.

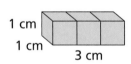

volume = 3 cubic centimeters

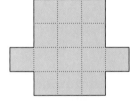

surface area = 14 square centimeters

In this investigation, you will explore the possible surface areas for a rectangular box that holds a given volume.

# 2.1 Packaging Blocks

ATC Toy Company is planning to market a set of children's alphabet blocks. Each block is a cube with 1-inch edges, so each block has a volume of 1 cubic inch.

## Problem 2.1 Finding Surface Area

The company wants to arrange 24 blocks in the shape of a rectangular prism and then package them in a box that exactly fits the prism.

**A.** Find all the ways 24 cubes can be arranged into a rectangular prism. Make a sketch of each arrangement. Record the dimensions and surface area. It may help to organize your findings into a table like the one below:

### Possible Arrangements of 24 Cubes

| Length | Width | Height | Volume | Surface Area | Sketch |
|--------|-------|--------|--------|--------------|--------|
| ▪ | ▪ | ▪ | ▪ | ▪ | ▪ |
| ▪ | ▪ | ▪ | ▪ | ▪ | ▪ |
| ▪ | ▪ | ▪ | ▪ | ▪ | ▪ |

**B.** Which of your arrangements requires the box made with the least material? Which requires the box made with the most material?

**C.** Which arrangement would you recommend to ATC Toy Company? Explain why.

**D.** Why do you think the company makes 24 alphabet blocks rather than 26?

ACE Homework starts on page 24.

You discovered that 24 blocks can be packaged in different ways that use varying amounts of packaging material. By using less material, a company can save money, reduce waste, and conserve natural resources.

Which rectangular arrangement of cubes uses the least amount of packaging material?

Problem **2.2** **Finding the Least Surface Area**

**A.** Explore the possible arrangements of each of the following numbers of cubes. Find the arrangement that requires the least amount of packaging material.

**1.** 8 cubes          **2.** 27 cubes          **3.** 12 cubes

**B. 1.** Make a conjecture about the rectangular arrangement of cubes that requires the least packaging material.

**2.** Does your conjecture work for 30 cubes? Does it work for 64 cubes? If not, change your conjecture so it works for any number of cubes. When you have a conjecture that you think is correct, give reasons why you think your conjecture is valid.

**C.** Describe a strategy for finding the total surface area of a closed box.

**ACE** Homework starts on page 24.

Area is expressed in square units, such as square inches or square centimeters. You can abbreviate square units by writing the abbreviation for the unit followed by a raised 2. For example, an abbreviation for square inches is in.$^2$.

Volume is expressed in cubic units. You can abbreviate cubic units by writing the abbreviation for the unit followed by a raised 3. For example, an abbreviation for cubic centimeters is cm$^3$.

### Getting Ready for Problem 2.3

One seventh-grade student, Bernie, wonders if he can compare volumes without having to calculate them exactly. He figures that volume measures the contents of a container. He fills the prism on the left with rice and then pours the rice into the one on the right.

- How can you decide if there is enough rice or too much rice to fill the prism on the right?

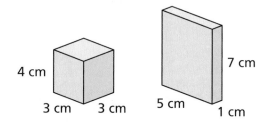

# 2.3 Filling Rectangular Boxes

**A** company may have boxes custom-made to package its products. However, a company may also buy ready-made boxes. The Save-a-Tree packaging company sells ready-made boxes in several sizes.

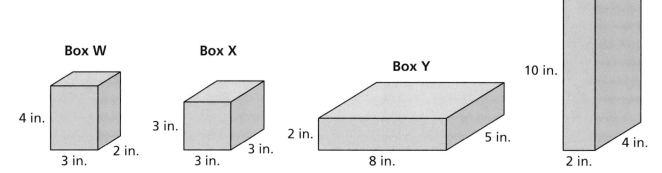

ATC Toy Company is considering using Save-a-Tree's Box Z to ship alphabet blocks. Each block is a 1-inch cube. ATC needs to know how many blocks will fit into Box Z and the surface area of the box.

**A.** The number of unit cubes that fit in a box is the volume of the box.

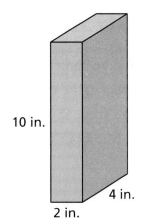

10 in.

4 in.

2 in.

    **1.** How many cubes will fit in a single layer at the bottom of this box?

    **2.** How many identical layers can be stacked in this box?

    **3.** What is the total number of cubes that can be packed in this box?

    **4.** Consider the number of cubes in each layer, the number of layers, the volume, and the dimensions of the box. What connections do you see among these measurements?

**B.** Find the surface area of Box Z.

**C.** Suppose Box Z is put down on its side so its base is 4 inches by 10 inches and its height is 2 inches. Does this affect the volume of the box? Does this affect the surface area? Explain your reasoning.

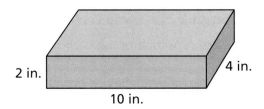

2 in.

4 in.

10 in.

**D.** Apply your strategies for finding volume and surface area to Boxes W, X, and Y.

ACE Homework starts on page 24.

## Applications

**In Exercises 1–3, rectangular prisms are made using 1-inch cubes.**

    **a.** Find the length, width, and height of each prism.

    **b.** Find the amount of material needed to make a box for each prism.

    **c.** Find the number of cubes in each prism.

**1.**

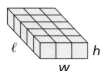

**2.**

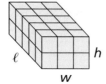

**3.**

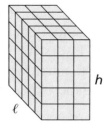

**4.** Suppose you plan to make a box that will hold exactly 40 one-inch cubes.

    **a.** Give the dimensions of all the possible boxes you can make.

    **b.** Which box has the least surface area? Which box has the greatest surface area?

    **c.** Why might you want to know the dimensions of the box with the least surface area?

**5.** Each of these boxes holds 36 ping-pong balls.

12 cm

12 cm

12 cm

4 cm

    **a.** Without figuring, which box has the least surface area? Why?

    **b.** Check your guess by finding the surface area of each box.

**6. a.** The box at the right is a $6 \times 2 \times 1$ arrangement of drink cans. Suppose the dimensions of the box are, in centimeters, $39 \times 13 \times 12.25$. Compare the surface area of the box with the more traditional $4 \times 3 \times 1$ arrangement, which measures, in centimeters, $26 \times 19.5 \times 12.25$.

**b.** The box at the right is a $4 \times 3 \times 2$ arrangement of drink cans. Suppose the dimensions of the box are, in centimeters, $26 \times 19.5 \times 24.5$. Compare the surface area of the box with the more traditional $6 \times 4 \times 1$ arrangement, which measures, in centimeters, $39 \times 26 \times 12.25$.

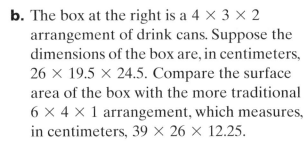

**7. a.** Sketch a rectangular box with dimensions 2 centimeters by 7 centimeters by 3 centimeters.

**b.** What is the surface area of the box?

**c.** Draw a net for the box on grid paper. What is the relationship between the area of the net and the surface area of the box?

**In Exercises 8–10, rectangular prisms are drawn using inch cubes.**

**a.** Find the length, width, and height of each prism.

**b.** Find the volume of each prism. Describe how you found the volume.

**c.** Find the surface area of each prism. Describe how you found the surface area.

**8.**

**9.**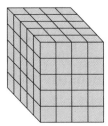

**10.**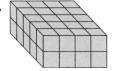

**11. a.** What is the total number of cubes, including the cubes already shown, needed to fill the closed box below?

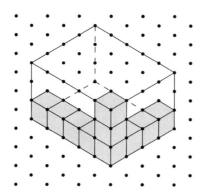

**b.** What is the surface area of the box?

**For Exercises 12–14, find the volume and surface area of the closed box.**

**12.**
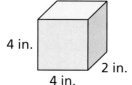
4 in.
2 in.
4 in.

**13.**
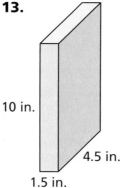
10 in.
4.5 in.
1.5 in.

**14.**
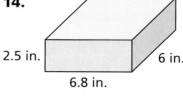
2.5 in.
6 in.
6.8 in.

**15. a.** Make a sketch of a closed box with dimensions 2 centimeters by 3 centimeters by 5 centimeters.

**b.** How many centimeter cubes will fit in one layer at the bottom of the box?

**c.** How many layers are needed to fill the box?

**d.** Find the volume of the box.

**e.** Find the surface area of the box.

**16.** Mr. Turner's classroom is 20 feet wide, 30 feet long, and 10 feet high.

**a.** Sketch a scale model of the classroom. Label the dimensions of the classroom on your sketch.

**Go Online**
PHSchool.com
**For:** Multiple-Choice Skills Practice
**Web Code:** ana-6254

**b.** Find the volume of the classroom. Why might this information be useful?

**c.** Find the total area of the walls, the floor, and the ceiling. Why might this information be useful?

**17.** Each expression below will help you to find the volume or surface area of one of the boxes pictured. Simplify each expression. Decide whether you have found a volume or a surface area, and for which box.

**Homework Help Online**
PHSchool.com
**For:** Help with Exercise 17
**Web Code:** ane-6217

**a.** $2 \times (3.5 \times 5.7) + 2 \times (5.7 \times 12) + 2 \times (3.5 \times 12)$

**b.** $6\frac{1}{4} \times 6$     **c.** $6 \times 6\frac{1}{2}$     **d.** $2\frac{1}{3} \times 2\frac{2}{5} \times 5$

**Box B**

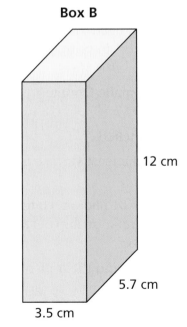

**Box A**

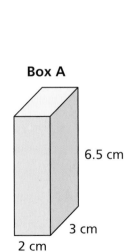

12 cm

5.7 cm

3.5 cm

6.5 cm

3 cm

2 cm

**Box C**

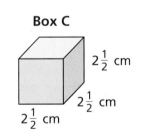

$2\frac{1}{2}$ cm

$2\frac{1}{2}$ cm

$2\frac{1}{2}$ cm

**Box D**

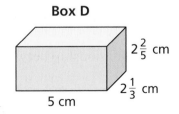

$2\frac{2}{5}$ cm

$2\frac{1}{3}$ cm

5 cm

**18.** The city of Centerville plans to dig a rectangular landfill. The landfill will have a base with dimensions 700 ft by 200 ft and a depth of 85 ft.

   **a.** How many cubic feet of garbage will the landfill hold?

   **b.** What information do you need to determine how long the landfill can be used until it is full?

   **c.** Centerville hires an excavator to dig the hole for the landfill. How many cubic yards of dirt will he have to haul away?

**19.** Describe the dimensions of a rectangular prism with a volume of 80 cubic inches but a surface area of less than 132 square inches.

# Connections

**20. a.** There is only one way to arrange five identical cubes into the shape of a rectangular prism. Sketch the rectangular prism made from five identical cubes.

   **b.** Find more numbers of cubes that can be arranged into a rectangular prism in only one way. What do these numbers have in common?

**21. a.** Sketch every rectangular prism that can be made from ten identical cubes.

   **b.** Find the surface area of each prism you sketched.

   **c.** Give the dimensions of the prism that has the least surface area.

**22. a.** Each of the boxes you designed in Problem 2.1 had a rectangular base and a height. Use a graph to show the relationship between the area of the base and the height of each box.

   **b.** Describe the relationship between the height and the area of the base.

   **c.** How might your graph be useful to a packaging engineer at ATC Toy Company?

**23.** The dimensions of the recreation center floor are 150 ft by 45 ft, and the walls are 10 ft high. A gallon of paint will cover 400 ft². About how much paint is needed to paint the walls of the recreation center?

**24.** If a small can of paint will cover 1,400 square inches, about how many small cans are needed to paint the walls of the recreation center described in Exercise 23?

**For Exercises 25–27, use the three given views of a three-dimensional building to sketch the building. Then, find its volume.**

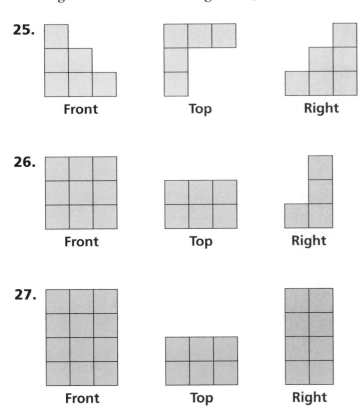

**25.**
Front   Top   Right

**26.**
Front   Top   Right

**27.**
Front   Top   Right

# Extensions

**28.** Many drinks are packaged in rectangular boxes of 24 cans.

   **a.** During the spring of 1993, a company announced that it was going to package 24 twelve-ounce cans into a more cube-like shape. Why might the company have decided to change their packaging?

   **b.** List all the ways 24 twelve-ounce cans of soda can be arranged and packaged in a rectangular box. Which arrangement do you recommend that a drink company use? Why?

**29.** Slam Dunk Sporting Goods packages its basketballs in cubic boxes with 1-foot edges. For shipping, the company packs 12 basketballs (in its boxes) into a large rectangular shipping box.

   **a.** Find the dimensions of every possible shipping box into which the boxes of basketballs would exactly fit.

   **b.** Find the surface area of each shipping box in part (a).

   **c.** Slam Dunk uses the shipping box that requires the least material. Which shipping box does it use?

   **d.** Slam Dunk decides to ship basketballs in boxes of 24. It wants to use the shipping box that requires the least material. Find the dimensions of the box it should use. How much more packaging material is needed to ship 24 basketballs than to ship 12 basketballs?

# Mathematical Reflections 2

In this investigation, you arranged cubes in the shape of rectangular prisms, and you also found the arrangements with the least and greatest surface area. You developed methods for finding surface area and volume. These questions will help you summarize what you have learned.

Think about your answers to these questions. Discuss your ideas with other students and your teacher. Then write a summary of your findings in your notebook.

1. For a given number of cubes, what arrangement will give a rectangular prism with the least surface area? What arrangement will give a rectangular prism with the greatest surface area? Use specific examples to illustrate your ideas.

2. Describe how you can find the surface area of a rectangular prism. Give a rule for finding the surface area.

3. Describe how you can find the volume of any prism. Give a rule for finding the volume.

# Prisms and Cylinders

**I**n Investigation 2, you found the volume of rectangular prisms by filling the prism with cubes. The number of cubes in the bottom layer is the same as the area of the rectangular base and the number of layers is the height. To find the volume, you multiply the area of the base ($\ell \times w$) times its height $h$, so that $V = \ell w h$.

A **prism** is a three-dimensional shape with a top and a base that are congruent polygons, and *lateral* (side) faces that are parallelograms. Each prism is named for the shape of its base. The boxes we have seen so far in this unit are rectangular prisms. A triangular prism has a triangular base.

A **cylinder** is a three-dimensional shape with a top and base that are congruent circles.

The prisms and cylinder below all have the same height.

*Suppose you filled the triangular prism with rice and poured the rice into each of the other cylinders. How do you think the volumes would compare? What about the surface areas?*

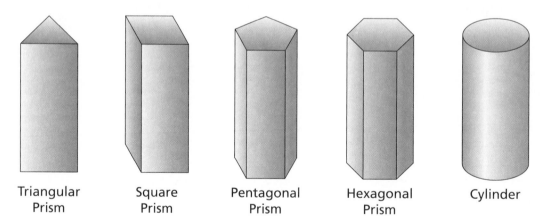

| Triangular Prism | Square Prism | Pentagonal Prism | Hexagonal Prism | Cylinder |

## 3.1 Filling Fancy Boxes

**I**n this problem you will explore prisms with bases that are not rectangles. You will start by making models of prisms.

**Directions for Making Paper Prisms** (These paper models are open at the top and bottom.)

- Start with four identical sheets of paper.
- Use the shorter dimension as the height for each prism.
- Make a *triangular* prism by marking and folding one of the sheets of paper into three congruent rectangles. Tape the paper into the shape of a triangular prism.

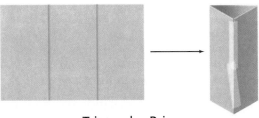

Triangular Prism

- Make a *square* prism by marking, folding, and taping a sheet of paper into four congruent rectangles.
- Make a *pentagonal* prism by marking, folding, and taping a sheet of paper into five congruent rectangles.
- Make a *hexagonal* prism by marking, folding, and taping a sheet of paper into six congruent rectangles.

## Problem 3.1 Finding the Volumes of Other Prisms

**A.** In your group, follow the directions above. (Keep your models for Problem 3.2.)

**B.** How do the volumes of the prisms compare as the number of faces in the prisms increases? Does the volume remain the same? Explain.

**C.** Consider the number of cubes you need to cover the base as one layer. Next, think about the total number of layers of cubes needed to fill the prism. Does this seem like a reasonable method for computing the volume of each prism?

**D.** Suppose that each of your paper prisms has a top and a bottom. As the number of faces of a prism (with the same height) increases, what happens to the surface area of the prisms? Are the surface areas of the prisms the same? Explain your reasoning.

ACE Homework starts on page 38.

# 3.2 Filling Cylinders

The last problem revealed some interesting connections among volume and surface area of prisms. A cylinder resembles a many-sided prism. In this problem you will explore cylinders and use what you have already learned about prisms to find the volume and surface area of a cylinder.

**Directions for Making Paper Cylinders**

- Start with two identical sheets of paper.
- Use the longer dimension of one sheet of paper as the height of the first cylinder. Tape the paper into the shape of a cylinder.
- Use the shorter dimension of the other sheet of paper as the height of the second cylinder. Tape the paper into the shape of a cylinder.

*How do the volumes of the two cylinders compare?*

You need an efficient way to compute the volume of a cylinder. In Problem 3.1 you found the volume of a prism by counting the number of cubes that fit in a single layer at the base and then counting the number of layers it would take to fill the prism. Let's see if a similar approach will work for cylinders.

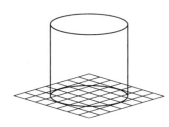  

Trace the base.      How many cubes would fit in one layer?      How many layers would it take to fill the cylinder?

As with rectangular prisms, the bottom of any prism or cylinder is called the base.

# Problem 3.2 Finding the Volumes of Cylinders

**A.** Copy the circles at the right onto inch graph paper. With two identical sheets of paper, make two models of cylinders with open tops and bases that match the bases drawn on the grid paper.

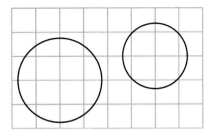

**active math online**
**For:** Virtual Cylinder Activity
**Visit:** PHSchool.com
**Web Code:** and-6302

**B.** Predict which of the two cylinders has the greater volume.

**C. 1.** How many inch cubes fit on the bottom layer of each cylinder?

    **2.** How many layers of inch cubes are needed to fill each cylinder?

    **3.** What is the total number of inch cubes needed to fill each cylinder?

    **4.** How can the dimensions help you calculate the volume of each cylinder?

**D.** Suppose Cylinder 1 has a height of 10 centimeters and a radius of 4 centimeters and Cylinder 2 has a height of 4 centimeters and a radius of 10 centimeters. Are the volumes equal? Explain.

**E.** Suppose that each of your paper cylinders had a top and a bottom. Describe how you could find the surface area of each cylinder.

**ACE** Homework starts on page 38.

# 3.3 Making Cylinders and Prisms from Nets

**T**he distance from the base of a cylinder to the top is called the height. You can describe a cylinder by giving its dimensions.

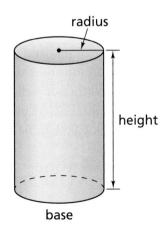

radius

height

base

Draw nets like the following on centimeter grid paper.

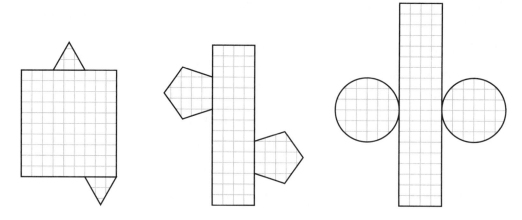

**A.** What is the surface area of each shape? Explain your reasoning.

**B.** Cut out your nets. Tape the pieces of the nets together to form a cylinder or a prism.

    **1.** Describe how to find the surface area of any prism or cylinder.

    **2.** Describe how the dimensions of a cylinder help you to find its surface area.

**C. 1.** Find the volume of each prism and cylinder.

    **2.** Compare the methods for finding the volume of a prism and finding the volume of a cylinder.

**ACE** Homework starts on page 38.

## Did You Know?

The volume, or capacity, of a liquid container is often given in units like quarts, gallons, liters, and milliliters. These volumes do not tell you how many unit cubes each container will hold, but are based on cubic measures. For example, a gallon equals 231 cubic inches, a milliliter equals a cubic centimeter, and a liter is 1,000 cubic centimeters.

**Go Online**
PHSchool.com   **For:** Information about capacities
           **Web Code:** ane-9031

# 3.4 Making a New Juice Container

**active math**
**online**

**For:** Pouring and Filling
Activity
**Visit:** PHSchool.com
**Web Code:** and-6304

**F**ruit Tree Juice Company packages its most popular drink, apple-prune juice, in cylindrical cans. Each can is 8 centimeters high and has a radius of 2 centimeters.

Recent reports indicate a decline in the sales of Fruit Tree juice. At the same time, sales of juice sold by a competitor, the Wrinkled Prune Company, are on the rise. Market researchers at Fruit Tree determine that Wrinkled Prune's success is due to its new rectangular juice boxes. Fruit Tree decides to package its juice in rectangular boxes.

## Problem 3.4 Comparing Volumes

Fruit Tree wants the new rectangular box to have the same volume as the current cylindrical can.

**A. 1.** On centimeter grid paper, make a net for a box that will hold the same amount of juice as the cylindrical can. Cut out your net. When you are finished, fold and tape your pattern to form a rectangular box.

   **2.** Give the dimensions of your juice box. Are there other possibilities for the dimensions? Explain.

   **3.** Compare your juice box with the boxes made by your classmates. Which rectangular box shape do you think would make the best juice container? Why?

**B.** Compare the surface area of the cylindrical can with the surface area of your juice box. Which container has greater surface area?

ACE Homework starts on page 38.

## Applications

**1.** Cut a sheet of paper in half so you have two identical half-sheets of paper. Tape the long sides of one sheet together to form a cylinder. Tape the short sides from the second sheet together to form another cylinder. Suppose that each cylinder has a top and a bottom.

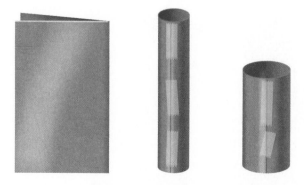

**a.** Which cylinder has the greater volume? Explain.

**b.** Which cylinder has the greater surface area? Explain.

**2.** A cylinder has a radius of 3 centimeters. Sand is poured into the cylinder to form a layer 1 centimeter deep.

**a.** What is the volume of sand in the cylinder?

**b.** Suppose the height of the cylinder is 20 centimeters. How many 1-centimeter deep layers of sand are needed to fill the cylinder?

**c.** What is the volume of the cylinder?

**3.** Find a cylindrical object in your home or school. Record the dimensions and find the volume of the cylinder.

**For Exercises 4–6, decide whether you have found an area, a surface area, or a volume. Then, identify whether the computation relates to Figure 1, 2, or 3.**

**4.** $\left(\frac{1}{2} \times \frac{1}{2} \times \pi \times 2\right) + \left(2 \times \frac{1}{2} \times \pi \times 5\right)$

**5.** $3 \times 3 \times \pi$

**6.** $1 \times 1 \times \pi \times 3$

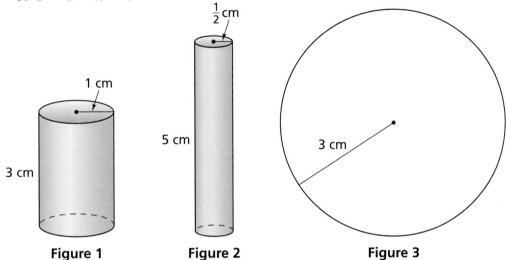

Figure 1          Figure 2          Figure 3

**7.** A pipeline carrying oil is 5,000 kilometers long and has an inside diameter of 20 centimeters.

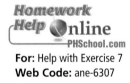

**For:** Help with Exercise 7
**Web Code:** ane-6307

    **a.** How many cubic centimeters of oil will it take to fill 1 kilometer of the pipeline? (1 km = 100,000 cm)

    **b.** How many cubic centimeters of oil will it take to fill the entire pipeline?

**8.** What feature of a cylinder uses the given units?

   **a.** centimeters

   **b.** square centimeters

   **c.** cubic centimeters

**For Exercises 9–11, find the volume of each cylinder.**

   **9.** height = 10 centimeters, radius = 6.5 centimeters

   **10.** height = 6.5 centimeters, radius = 10 centimeters

   **11.** height = 12 inches, area of the base = 200 square inches

**Go Online**
PHSchool.com
**For:** Multiple-Choice Skills Practice
**Web Code:** ana-6354

**12.** Find the surface area of each closed cylinder in Exercises 9 and 10.

**13.** **a.** Will all rectangular prisms with the same height and base area have the same shape? Explain.

   **b.** Will all cylinders with the same height and base area have the same shape? Explain.

**14.** A cylindrical storage tank has a radius of 15 feet and a height of 30 feet.

   **a.** Make a sketch of the tank and label its dimensions.

   **b.** Find the volume of the tank.

   **c.** Find the surface area of the tank.

**15.** **a.** Sketch two different prisms, each with a base of area 40 square centimeters and a height of 5 centimeters.

   **b.** Find the volumes of your prisms.

   **c.** Do you think everyone in your class drew the same prisms? Explain.

   **d.** Do you think all the prisms have the same volumes as your prisms? Explain.

**16.** Below are side and top views of a triangular prism with bases that are equilateral triangles.

   **a.** What is the volume of this prism? How did you find the volume?

   **b.** What is the surface area? How did you find the surface area?

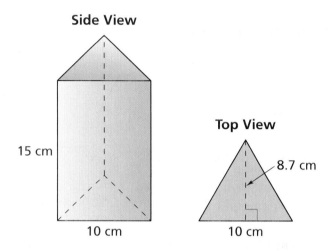

**Side View**

15 cm

10 cm

**Top View**

8.7 cm

10 cm

**17.** Below is a scale model of a net for a cylinder.

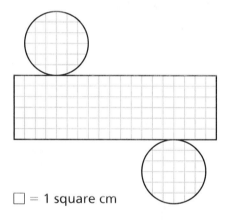

☐ = 1 square cm

   **a.** Suppose the net is assembled. Find the volume of the cylinder.

   **b.** Find the surface area of the cylinder.

**18.** Which container below has the greater volume? Greater surface area?

A *closed rectangular prism* whose height is 12 centimeters, width is 3 centimeters, and length is 4 centimeters.

A *closed cylinder* whose height is 12 centimeters and diameter is 3 centimeters.

**19.** The bases of the prisms you made in Problem 3.1 are shown at the right. Each prism has a height of 8.5 inches.

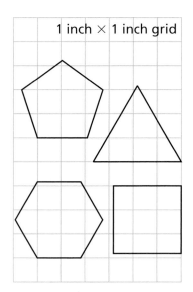

1 inch × 1 inch grid

   **a.** Compute the volume of each prism.

   **b.** Compare these volumes with those you found in Problem 3.1.

**20.** Carlos wants to build a circular hot tub with a volume of 1,000 cubic feet. What is a good approximation for the radius of the tub?

**21.** Carlos decides he would rather build a rectangular hot tub that is 4 feet high and holds 400 cubic feet of water. What could the dimensions of the base of Carlos's hot tub be?

**22.** A popcorn vendor needs to order popcorn boxes. The vendor must decide between a cylindrical box and a rectangular box.

- The cylindrical box has a height of 20 centimeters and a radius of 7 centimeters.

- The rectangular box has a height of 20 centimeters and a square base with 12-centimeter sides.

- The price of each box is based on the amount of material needed to make the box.

- The vendor plans to charge $2.75 for popcorn, regardless of the shape of the box.

   **a.** Make a sketch of each box. Label the dimensions.

   **b.** Find the volume and surface area of each box.

   **c.** Which box would you choose? Give the reasons for your choice. What additional information might help you make a better decision?

# Connections

**23.** Serge and Jorge were talking about the number $\pi$. Serge said that any problem involving $\pi$ had to be about circles. Jorge disagreed and showed him the example below. What do you think?

1 inch

$\pi$ inches

**24.** The Buy-and-Go Mart sells drinks in three sizes. Which size gives the most ounces of drink per dollar? Explain.

| Small | Medium | Large |
|:---:|:---:|:---:|
| 12 oz. | 18 oz. | 32 oz. |
| $1.25 | $1.75 | $3.00 |

**25. a.** Identify objects at school that are shaped like prisms, one rectangular and one or two non-rectangular prisms.

   **b.** Without measuring, estimate the volume of each object.

   **c.** How can you check the volumes you found in part (b)?

**26.** A drink can is a cylinder with radius 3 centimeters and height 12 centimeters. Ms. Doyle's classroom is 6 meters wide, 8 meters long, and 3 meters high. Estimate the number of drink cans that would fit inside Ms. Doyle's classroom. Explain your estimate.

**27. a.** Make a table showing the relationship between the diameter and the circumference of a circle. Include data for diameters 1, 2, 3, . . . 10 centimeters. Use this table for parts (b)–(d).

**b.** Graph the data in your table.

**c.** Suppose that each of the circles represented in your table is the base of a cylinder with height of 2 centimeters. Some of these cylinders are sketched below. Make a table to show the relationship between the diameter of the base and the volume of the cylinder.

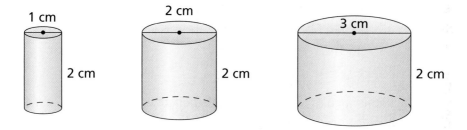

**d.** Make a graph of the volume data.

**e.** Compare the graphs of parts (b) and (d). How are they alike? How are they different?

**28.** Some take-out drink containers have a circular top and bottom that are not congruent. How can you estimate the volume of the container below?

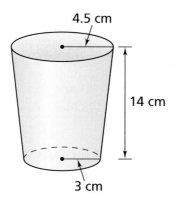

**29.** Leo has two prism-shaped containers. One has a volume of $3\frac{3}{4}$ cubic feet and the other has a volume of $\frac{1}{3}$ cubic feet.

**a.** How many of the smaller prisms would it take to fill the larger prism?

**b.** What operation did you use to find the answer? Explain.

**30.** Emily has two prism-shaped containers. One has a volume of $2\frac{2}{5}$ cubic feet, and the other has a volume of $\frac{2}{3}$ cubic feet.

**a.** How many of the smaller prisms would it take to fill the larger prism?

**b.** What operation did you use to find the answer? Explain.

**31.** The diagram shows a fish tank after a container of water is poured into the tank.

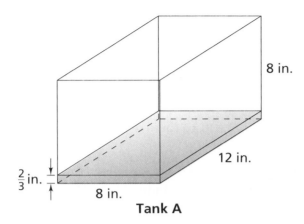

8 in.

12 in.

$\frac{2}{3}$ in.

8 in.

**Tank A**

**a.** How many containers of water are needed to fill the tank?

**b.** What fraction of the tank does the container fill?

**c.** A different container holds $12\frac{3}{4}$ cubic inches of water. How many of these containers are needed to fill the tank?

**32.** The diagram shows a fish tank after a container of water is poured into the tank.

4 in.

15 in.

$1\frac{3}{5}$ in.

5 in.

**Tank B**

**a.** How many containers of water are needed to fill the tank?

**b.** What fraction of the tank does the container fill?

**c.** A different container holds $4\frac{4}{9}$ cubic inches of water. How many of these containers are needed to fill the tank?

# Extensions

**33.** A cylindrical can is packed securely in a box as shown at the right.

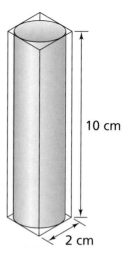

   **a.** Find the radius and height of the can.

   **b.** What is the volume of the empty space between the can and the box?

   **c.** Find the ratio of the volume of the can to the volume of the box.

   **d.** Make up a similar example with a can and a box of different sizes. What is the ratio of the volume of your can to the volume of your box? How does the ratio compare with the ratio you found in part (c)?

**34. a.** The drawing at the right shows a prism with an odd-shaped top and bottom and rectangular sides. The top and bottom each have an area of 10 square centimeters, and the height is 4 centimeters. What is the volume of the prism? Explain your reasoning.

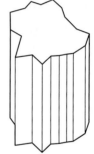

   **b.** Is your estimate for the volume more than, less than, or equal to the exact volume? Explain.

**35.** Suppose you know the height and volume of a cylinder. Can you make a net for the cylinder?

# Mathematical Reflections 3

**I**n this investigation, you developed methods for finding the volume and surface area of prisms and cylinders. These questions will help you summarize what you have learned.

Think about your answers to these questions. Discuss your ideas with other students and your teacher. Then write a summary of your findings in your notebook.

1. Describe how to find the volume of a rectangular prism.

2. **a.** Describe how you can find the volume of a cylinder using its dimensions. Write a rule that represents your strategy.

   **b.** Describe how you can find the surface area of a cylinder using its dimensions. Write a rule that represents your strategy.

3. Discuss the similarities and differences in the methods for finding the volume of a cylinder, a rectangular prism, and a non-rectangular prism.

4. Discuss the similarities and differences in the methods for finding the surface area of a cylinder, a rectangular prism, and a non-rectangular prism.

# Cones, Spheres, and Pyramids

**M**any common and important three-dimensional objects are not shaped like prisms or cylinders. For example, ice cream is often served in **cones.** The planet we live on is nearly a **sphere.** Many monuments here and in other countries are shaped like **pyramids.**

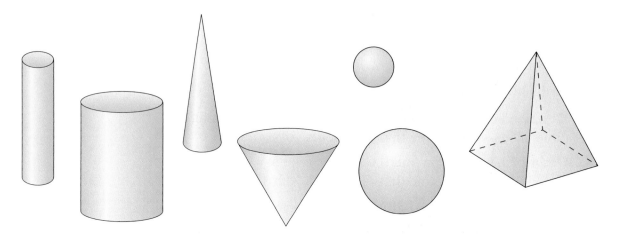

As with a cylinder and a prism, you can describe a cone or a square pyramid by giving its dimensions. The dimensions of a cone are the radius of its circular base and its height. The dimensions of a square pyramid are its length, width, and height.

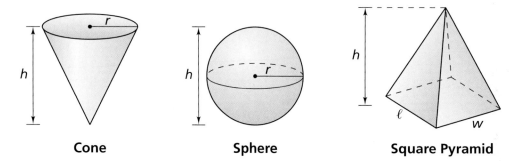

**Cone**          **Sphere**          **Square Pyramid**

Although spheres may differ in size, they are all the same shape. You can describe a sphere by giving its radius.

In this investigation, you will explore ways to determine the volumes of cones, pyramids, and spheres by looking for relationships between cones and pyramids and between cones and spheres.

# 4.1 Comparing Spheres and Cylinders

In this problem, you will make a sphere and a cylinder with the same diameter and the same height and then compare their volumes. (The height of a sphere is just its diameter.) You can use the relationship you observe to develop a method for finding the volume of a sphere.

## Did You Know?

Earth is nearly a sphere. You may have heard that, until Christopher Columbus's voyage in 1492, most people believed Earth was flat. Actually, as early as the fourth century B.C., scientists had figured out that Earth was round.

The scientists observed the shadow of Earth as it passed across the moon during a lunar eclipse. The shadow was round. Combining this observation with evidence gathered from observing constellations, these scientists concluded that Earth was spherical. In the third century B.C., Eratosthenes, a Greek mathematician, was actually able to estimate the circumference of Earth.

 Go Online
PHSchool.com **For:** Information about historical views of Earth's shape
**Web Code:** ane-9031

## Problem 4.1 Comparing Spheres and Cylinders

- Make a sphere from modeling clay. Measure its diameter.
- Make a cylinder with an open top and bottom from a sheet of stiff transparent plastic to fit snugly around your clay sphere. Trim the height of the cylinder to match the height of the sphere. This makes the diameter and the height of the cylinder equal to the diameter and the height of the sphere. Tape the cylinder together so that it remains rigid.

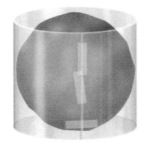

- Now, flatten the clay sphere so that it fits snugly in the bottom of the cylinder. Mark the height of the flattened sphere on the cylinder.

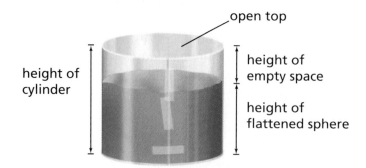

**A.** Measure and record the height of the cylinder, the height of the empty space, and the height of the flattened sphere. Use this information to find the volume of the cylinder and the original sphere.

**B.** What is the relationship between the volume of the sphere and the volume of the cylinder?

**C.** A cylinder with a height equal to its diameter has a volume of 48 cubic inches. How can you use the relationship in Question B to find the volume of a sphere whose radius is the same as the cylinder?

Remove the clay from the cylinder and save the cylinder for Problem 4.2.

**ACE** Homework starts on page 54.

# 4.2 Cones and Cylinders, Pyramids and Cubes

**I**n Problem 4.1, you discovered the relationship between the volume of a sphere and the volume of a cylinder. In this problem, you will look for the relationship between the volume of a cone and the volume of a cylinder, and between the volume of a pyramid and the volume of a square prism.

- Roll a piece of stiff paper into a cone shape so that the tip touches the bottom of the cylinder you made in Problem 4.1.

- Tape the cone shape along the seam. Trim the cone so that it is the same height as the cylinder.

- Fill the cone to the top with sand or rice, and empty the contents into the cylinder. Repeat this as many times as needed to fill the cylinder completely.

**A.** What is the relationship between the volume of the cone and the volume of the cylinder?

**B.** Suppose a cylinder, a cone, and a sphere have the same radius and the same height. What is the relationship between the volumes of the three shapes?

**C.** Suppose a cone, a cylinder, and a sphere all have the same height, and that the cylinder has a volume of 64 cubic inches. How do you use the relationship in Question B to find

**1.** the volume of a sphere whose radius is the same as the cylinder?

**2.** the volume of a cone whose radius is the same as the cylinder?

**D.** Suppose the radius of a cylinder, a cone, and a sphere is 5 centimeters and the height of the cylinder and cone is 8 centimeters. Find the volume of the cylinder, cone, and sphere.

**E. 1.** Use a square prism and a pyramid to conduct an experiment similar to the one on the previous page. The pyramid should have the same size base as the prism and the same height (shown at the right).

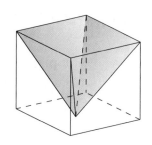

What is the relationship between the volume of the prism and the volume of the pyramid.

**2.** How are finding the volumes of the cones and pyramids alike?

 **Homework starts on page 54.**

# 4.3 Melting Ice Cream

Esther and Jasmine buy ice cream from Chilly's Ice Cream Parlor. They want to bring back an ice cream cone to Esther's little brother but decide the ice cream would melt before they got back home. Jasmine wonders, "If the ice cream all melts into the cone, will it fill the cone?"

### Problem 4.3 Comparing Volumes of Spheres, Cylinders, and Cones

Esther gets a scoop of ice cream in a cone, and Jasmine gets a scoop in a cylindrical cup. Each container has a height of 8 centimeters and a radius of 4 centimeters. Each scoop of ice cream is a sphere with a radius of 4 centimeters.

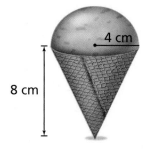

**A.** Suppose Jasmine allows her ice cream to melt. Will the melted ice cream fill her cup exactly? Explain.

**B.** Suppose Esther allows her ice cream to melt. Will the melted ice cream fill her cone exactly? Explain.

**C.** How many same-sized scoops of ice cream of the size shown on the previous page can be packed into each container?

**ACE** Homework starts on page 54.

Frank and Ernest

© 2002 Thaves. Reprinted with permission. Newspaper dist. by NEA, Inc.

You have looked at prisms, cylinders, cones, and spheres. Many three-dimensional objects do not have such regular shapes.

According to legend, Archimedes (ahr kuh MEE deez) made an important discovery while taking a bath in the third century B.C. He noticed that the water level rose when he sat down in a tub. This was because his body had *displaced* some water. He determined that he could find the weight of any floating object by finding the weight of the water that the object displaced.

It is said that Archimedes was so excited about his discovery that he jumped from his bath and, without dressing, ran into the streets shouting "Eureka!"

Go Online
PHSchool.com   **For:** Information about water displacement
**Web Code:** ane-9031

## Applications

1. A playground ball has a diameter of 18 cm.

   a. Sketch a cylinder that fits the playground ball, and label its height and base.

   b. What is the volume of the cylinder?

   c. What is the volume of the ball?

2. Find the volume of an exercise ball with a diameter of 62 centimeters.

**For Exercises 3–6, find the volume of the following spheres. In some spheres, the diameter is given. In others, the radius is given.**

3.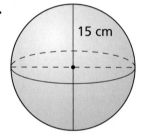
15 cm

4.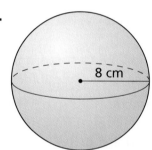
8 cm

5.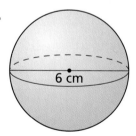
6 cm

6.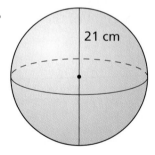
21 cm

**For Exercises 7–9, each of the number sentences models the formula for the volume of a figure you have worked with in this unit. Name the figure, sketch and label the figure, and find the volume.**

7. $2\frac{2}{3} \times 4\frac{4}{5} \times 3\frac{7}{8}$

8. $\pi \times (2.2)^2 \times 6.5$

9. $\frac{1}{3}\pi \times (4.25)^2 \times 10$

**10.** Watertown has three water storage tanks in different shapes: a cylinder, a cone, and a sphere. Each tank has a radius of 20 feet and a height of 40 feet.

    **a.** Sketch each tank, and label its dimensions.

    **b.** Estimate which tank will hold the most water. Explain.

    **c.** What is the volume of the cylindrical tank?

    **d.** What is the volume of the conical tank?

    **e.** What is the volume of the spherical tank?

**11.** Find the volume of each shape.

**Homework Help Online**
PHSchool.com
**For:** Help with Exercise 11
**Web Code:** ane-6411

**a.**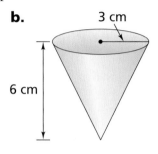
3 cm
6 cm

**b.**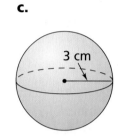
3 cm
6 cm

**c.**
3 cm

    **d.** How do the volumes of the three shapes compare?

**For Exercises 12 and 13, find the volume of each shape.**

**12.**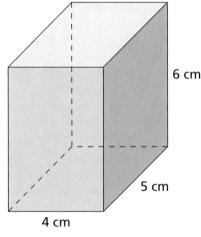
6 cm
5 cm
4 cm

**13.**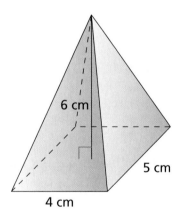
6 cm
5 cm
4 cm

**14. a.** Sketch and label the dimensions of a pyramid with base dimensions 5 centimeters by 7 centimeters and height 8 centimeters.

    **b.** Find the volume of the pyramid in part (a).

**15.** The track-and-field club is planning a frozen yogurt sale to raise money. They need to buy containers to hold the yogurt. They must choose between the cup and the cone below. Each container costs the same. The club plans to charge customers $1.25 for a serving of yogurt. Which container should the club buy? Why?

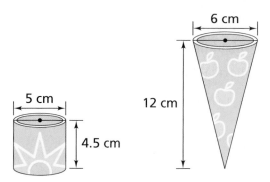

**16.** The Mathletes are planning their own frozen yogurt sale. They need to buy containers to hold the yogurt. They must choose between the prism and pyramid below. The other conditions that apply to the club in Exercise 15 also apply to the Mathletes. Which container should the club buy? Why?

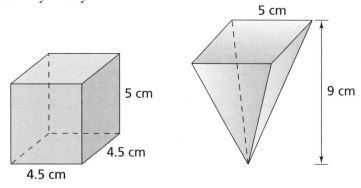

**17.** The prices and dimensions of several movie theater popcorn containers are shown below. Which container has the most popcorn per dollar? Explain. (Note: The diagrams below are not drawn to scale.)

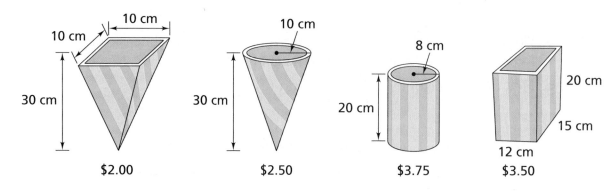

$2.00          $2.50          $3.75          $3.50

**For Exercises 18–20, the volume of each shape is approximately
250 cubic inches.**

**18.** Find the height of a cylinder with a radius of 3 inches.

**19.** Find the radius of a sphere.

**20.** Find the height of a cone with a radius of 3 inches.

**For Exercises 21–22, suppose each shape has a square base, the side of the
base is 3 inches, and the volume is 225 cubic inches. Find the height.**

**21.** rectangular prism  **22.** pyramid

**23.** If a scoop of ice cream is a sphere with a radius of 1 inch,
how many scoops can be packed into the cone at the right?

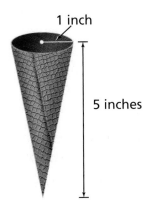

1 inch

5 inches

**24.** Chilly's Ice Cream Parlor purchases ice cream in $2\frac{1}{2}$-gallon
cylindrical containers. Each container is $10\frac{5}{32}$ inches high and
9 inches in diameter. A jumbo scoop of ice cream comes in the
shape of a sphere that is approximately 4 inches in diameter.
How many jumbo scoops can Chilly's serve from one
$2\frac{1}{2}$-gallon container of ice cream?

**25.** Chilly's Ice Cream Parlor is known for its root beer floats.

- The float is made by pouring root beer over 3 scoops of ice cream
  until the glass is filled $\frac{1}{2}$ inch from the top.

- A glass is in the shape of a cylinder with a radius of $1\frac{1}{4}$ inches and
  height of $8\frac{1}{2}$ inches.

- Each scoop of ice cream is a sphere with a radius of $1\frac{1}{4}$ inches.

Will there be more ice cream or more root beer in the float? Explain
your reasoning.

# Connections

**26.** A drink can is a cylinder with a radius of 3 centimeters and a height of 12 centimeters.

  **a.** Sketch the can, and label its dimensions.

  **b.** What is the circumference of the can?

  **c.** What is the volume?

  **d.** What is the surface area?

  **e.** How many cans will it take to fill a liter bottle? (A liter bottle contains 1,000 cubic centimeters.)

**27.** Three students measured the height of the same cylinder and their measurements are listed below. What is the average of the heights?

$2\frac{1}{2}$ feet $\qquad\qquad$ $2\frac{2}{3}$ feet $\qquad\qquad$ $2\frac{7}{12}$ feet

**For:** Multiple-Choice Skills Practice
**Web Code:** ana-6454

**28.** Five students measured the height of the same prism and their measurements are listed below. What is the average of the heights?

5.1 centimeters $\qquad\qquad$ 4.9 centimeters

5.25 centimeters $\qquad\qquad$ 5.15 centimeters

4.85 centimeters

**Each number sentence in Exercises 29–31 is a model for the surface area of a three-dimensional figure. Identify which three-dimensional figure the number sentence describes. Find the surface area.**

**29.** $2 \times (4) + 2 \times (8.5) + 2 \times (7.25)$

**30.** $2 \times (4 + 8.5 + 7.25)$

**31.** $2\pi \times (4)^2 + 2\pi \times (4)(8.5)$

**32.** Kaiya measures the circumference of a sphere and finds that it is 54 centimeters. What is the volume of the sphere?

# Extensions

**33.** Ted made a scale model of a submarine for his science class.

   **a.** What is the volume of Ted's model?

   **b.** If 1 inch in the model represents 20 feet in the actual submarine, what is the volume of the actual submarine?

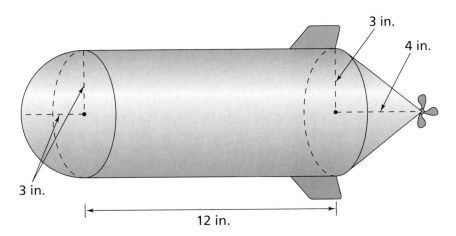

**34.** Some of the Inuit people build igloos shaped like hemispheres (halves of a sphere). Some of the Hopi people in Arizona build adobes shaped like rectangular boxes. Suppose an igloo has an inner diameter of 20 feet.

   **a.** Describe the shape of a Hopi dwelling that would provide the same amount of living space as the igloo described above.

   **b.** What dimensions of the floor would give the Hopi dwelling the same amount of floor space as the igloo?

**35.** A pyramid is named for the shape of its base. The left shape below is a triangular pyramid, the center shape is a square pyramid, and the right shape is a pentagonal pyramid.

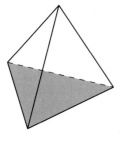 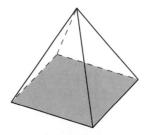 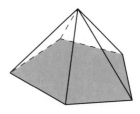

   **a.** Suppose the bases of a pyramid are all regular polygons. What happens to the shape of the pyramid as the number of sides in the base increases?

   **b.** Describe a method for finding the surface area of a pyramid.

**36.** For each shape below, find the dimensions that will most closely fit inside a cubic box with 5-centimeter edges.

   **a.** sphere          **b.** cylinder          **c.** cone          **d.** pyramid

   **e.** Does a sphere, a cylinder, or a cone fit best inside the cubic box? That is, for which shape is there the least space between the shape and the box?

**37.** The edges of a cube measure 10 centimeters. Describe the dimensions of a cylinder and a cone with the same volume as the cube. Explain.

Which shape should I start with?

# Mathematical Reflections 4

**I**n this investigation, you studied the relationships between the volumes of a cone, a sphere, and a cylinder with the same radius and height. You also studied the relationship between a square pyramid and a rectangular prism with the same base and height. These questions will help you summarize what you have learned.

Think about your answers to these questions. Discuss your ideas with other students and your teacher. Then write a summary of your findings in your notebook.

**1. a.** If a cone, a cylinder, and a sphere have the same radius and height, describe the relationships among their volumes. Use examples and sketches to illustrate your answer.

   **b.** If you know the radius of a sphere, how can you find the volume?

   **c.** If you know the radius and height of a cone, how can you find the volume?

**2. a.** Suppose a square pyramid and a rectangular prism have the same base and height. How do their volumes compare? Use examples and sketches to support your answer.

   **b.** Suppose you know the dimensions of the base and the height of a rectangular pyramid. How could you find the volume?

**3. a.** How are pyramids and cones alike and different?

   **b.** How are prisms and cylinders alike and different?

# Scaling Boxes

The cost of packaging materials and finding enough landfill for garbage and waste materials is becoming a problem for many communities. Some communities are looking at composting as a way to recycle garbage into productive soil.

Composting is a method for turning organic waste into rich soil. Today, many people have compost boxes that break down kitchen waste quickly and with little odor. The secret is in the worms!

**Recipe for a 1-2-3 Compost Box**

- Start with an open rectangular wood box that is 1 foot high, 2 feet wide, and 3 feet long. This is a 1-2-3 box.

- Mix 10 pounds of shredded newspaper with 15 quarts of water. Put the mixture in the 1-2-3 box.

- Add a few handfuls of soil.

- Add about 1,000 redworms (about 1 pound).

Every day, mix collected kitchen waste with the soil in the box. The worms will do the rest of the work, turning the waste into new soil. A 1-2-3 box will decompose about 0.5 pound of garbage each day.

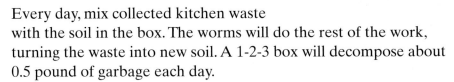

# 5.1 Building a Bigger Box

**D**eshondra chose composting as the topic of her science project. She plans to build a compost box at home and to keep records of the amount of soil produced over several weeks. She estimates that her family throws away 1 pound of garbage a day.

## Problem 5.1 Doubling the Volume of a Rectangular Prism

Deshondra wants to build a box that will decompose twice the amount of the 1-2-3 box.

**A.** Using grid paper, make scale models of a 1-2-3 box that will decompose 0.5 pound of garbage per day and a box that will decompose 1 pound of garbage per day.

**B. 1.** What are the dimensions of the new box?

    **2.** How many of the original boxes will fit into the new box?

    **3.** How is the volume of the new box related to the volume of the original box?

**C.** How much plywood is needed to construct an open 1-pound box?

**ACE** Homework starts on page 67.

# 5.2 Scaling Up the Compost Box

**I**n *Stretching and Shrinking,* you studied similar two-dimensional figures. The ideas you learned also apply to three-dimensional figures. For example, two rectangular prisms are similar if the ratios of the lengths of corresponding edges are equal. A 2-4-6 box is similar to the 1-2-3 box.

The *scale factor* is the number that each dimension of one rectangular prism must be multiplied by to get the dimensions of a similar prism. The scale factor from the 1-2-3 box to the 2-4-6 box is 2 because each edge length of the 1-2-3 box must be multiplied by 2 to get the corresponding edge length of the 2-4-6 box.

## Problem 5.2 Applying Scale Factors to Rectangular Prisms

Ms. Fernandez's class decides that building and maintaining a compost is a fascinating project. One student suggests that they could earn money selling worms and soil to a local nursery.

They decide to build different-sized boxes that are similar to the 1-2-3 box. They need to know how much material is needed to build the boxes and how much garbage each box will decompose in a day.

**A.** Copy and complete the table.

### Compost Box Project

| Open Box (h-w-ℓ) | Scale Factor | Surface Area (ft²) | Volume (ft³) | Amount of Garbage Decomposed in a Day | Number of Worms Needed |
|---|---|---|---|---|---|
| 1-2-3 | ■ | ■ | ■ | ■ | ■ |
| 2-4-6 | ■ | ■ | ■ | ■ | ■ |
| 3-6-9 | ■ | ■ | ■ | ■ | ■ |
| 4-8-12 | ■ | ■ | ■ | ■ | ■ |
| ■ | ■ | ■ | ■ | ■ | ■ |
| ■ | ■ | 1,024 | ■ | ■ | ■ |
| ■ | ■ | ■ | ■ | ■ | ■ |
| ■ | ■ | ■ | 6,000 | ■ | ■ |

**B.** How is the change in surface area from a 1-2-3 box to a similar box related to the scale factor from the 1-2-3 box to the similar box? Suppose the compost box has a top. Will your answer change? Explain.

**C.** How is the change in volume from a 1-2-3 box to a similar box related to the scale factor from the 1-2-3 box to the similar box? Explain.

**D.** How is the change in decomposed garbage related to the scale factor? Explain.

**E.** Suppose the scale factor between the 1-2-3 box and a similar box is N. Describe the dimensions, surface area, and volume of the similar box.

**ACE** Homework starts on page 67.

# 5.3 Building Model Ships

**B**uilders and architects often make models of cars, ships, buildings, and parks. A model is useful in determining several aspects of the building process, including structural strength, expense, and appearance.

Natasha builds a model ship from a kit. She tries to picture what the actual ship looks like. The scale factor from the model to the actual ship is 200.

**A.**  **1.** If the length of the model is 25 centimeters, what is the length of the actual ship?

   **2.** If the length of the flagpole on the actual ship is 30 meters, what is the length of the flagpole on the model?

**B.** The area of a rectangular floor on the model is 20 square centimeters. What is the area of the floor on the actual ship?

**C.** The cylindrical smoke stack on the model has a height of 4 centimeters and a radius of 1.5 centimeters.

   **1.** What are the dimensions of the smoke stack on the actual ship?

   **2.** What is the volume of the smoke stack on the actual ship?

   **3.** What is the surface area of the smoke stack on the actual ship?

**ACE** | **Homework starts on page 67.**

Did You Know?

Most minerals occur naturally as crystals. Every crystal has an orderly, internal pattern of atoms, with a distinctive way of locking new atoms into that pattern. As the pattern repeats, larger similar-shaped crystals are formed. The shape of the resulting crystal, such as a cube (like salt) or a six-sided form (like a snowflake), is a similar crystal.

As crystals grow, differences in temperature and chemical composition cause fascinating variations. But you will rarely find in your backyard the perfectly shaped mineral crystals that you see in a museum. In order to readily show their geometric form and flat surfaces, crystals need ideal or controlled growing conditions as well as room to grow.

Go Online
PHSchool.com    **For:** Information about growing crystals    **Web Code:** ane-9031

## Applications

1. **a.** Make a sketch of an open 1-3-5 box. Label the edges of the box.

   **b.** Sketch three boxes that have twice the volume of a 1-3-5 box. Label each box with its dimensions.

   **c.** Are any of the three boxes in part (b) similar to the 1-3-5 box? Explain.

**For Exercises 2–4, find the volume and the surface area of each closed box.**

2. 1-2-2               3. 1.5-1.5-3               4. 2-4-1

**For Exercises 5–7, decide if each pair of cylinders are similar. For each pair of similar cylinders, describe how many times larger one is than the other.**

5. Cylinder 1: height = 10 centimeters, radius = 5 centimeters
   Cylinder 2: height = 5 centimeters, radius = 2.5 centimeters

6. Cylinder 1: height = 10 centimeters, radius = 5 centimeters
   Cylinder 2: height = 30 centimeters, radius = 15 centimeters

7. Cylinder 1: height = 10 centimeters, radius = 5 centimeters
   Cylinder 2: height = 15 centimeters, radius = 10 centimeters

8. **a.** Make a sketch of an open 2-2-3 box and an open 2-2-6 box. Label the edges of the boxes.

   **b.** Find the volume of each box in part (a).

   **c.** Find the surface area of each box in part (a).

   **d.** Suppose you want to adapt the 1-2-3 compost box recipe for the boxes in part (a). How many worms and how much paper and water would you need for each box?

9. **a.** Give the dimensions of a rectangular box that will decompose 5 pounds of garbage per day. Explain your reasoning.

   **b.** Is your box similar to the 1-2-3 box? Explain.

**10.** One cube has edges measuring 1 foot. A second cube has edges measuring 2 feet. A third cube has edges measuring 3 feet.

   **a.** Make scale drawings of the three cubes. For each cube, tell what length in the drawing represents 1 foot.

   **b.** Find the surface area of each cube.

   **c.** Describe what happens to the surface area of a cube when the edge lengths are doubled, tripled, quadrupled, and so on.

**11. a.** Find the volume of each cube in Exercise 10.

   **b.** Describe what happens to the volume of a cube when the edge lengths are doubled, tripled, quadrupled, and so on.

**For Exercises 12–14, decide if each pair of rectangular boxes is similar. For each pair of similar boxes, describe how many times larger one box is than the other box.**

**Homework**
**Help** Online
PHSchool.com

**For:** Help with
Exercises 12–14
**Web Code:** ane-6512

**12.** 1-2-5 and 3-6-15

**13.** 2-3-2 and 5-6-5

**14.** 2-1-4 and 3-1.5-6

**15.** In the United States, an average of 2.7 pounds of garbage per person is delivered to landfills each day. A cubic foot of compressed garbage weighs about 50 pounds.

   **a.** Estimate the amount of garbage produced by a family of four in one year.

   **b.** Estimate the amount of garbage produced by the families of a class of 20 students in one year. Assume each family has four people.

**16.** Each year the United States generates 450 million cubic yards of solid waste. Mr. Costello's classroom is 42 feet long, 30 feet wide, and 12 feet high. How many rooms of this size would be needed to hold all this garbage?

**17.** For every ton of paper that is recycled, about 17 trees and 3.3 cubic yards of landfill space are saved. In the United States, the equivalent of 500,000 trees are used each week to produce the Sunday papers. Suppose all the Sunday papers this week are made from recycled paper. How much landfill is saved?

**In Exercises 18 and 19, a company that specializes in creating models of buildings is hired to develop models of pools for the upcoming summer Olympics. The pools are rectangular prisms. The scale factor from the model to the actual pool is 120.**

**18. a.** The dimensions of the actual diving pool are 20 meters by 20 meters by 4.9 meters. What are the dimensions of the model diving pool?

   **b.** What is the capacity (volume) of the actual diving pool. What is the capacity of the model diving pool?

   **c.** What is the surface area of the actual diving pool? What is the surface area of the model diving pool? (Do not include the surface of the water.)

**19. a.** The planned water capacity of the pool used for water polo and swimming is 1,650 cubic meters. What is the capacity of the model pool?

   **b.** A sunken corridor with viewing windows is planned for the diving pool. The area of a window in the actual setting is 160 square feet. What is the area of the window on the model?

# Connections

20. For parts (a)–(e), find the measure that makes a true statement.

   **a.** 1 square foot = ■ square inches

   **b.** 1 square yard = ■ square inches

   **c.** 1 cubic yard = ■ cubic feet

   **d.** 2 square yards = ■ square inches

   **e.** 3 square yards = ■ square inches

   **f.** For parts (a), (b), and (e) above, draw a diagram to justify your answer.

Go Online
PHSchool.com

For: Multiple-Choice Skills
     Practice
Web Code: ana-6554

**For Exercises 21–23, find the measure that makes a true statement.**

21. 4 square meters = ■ square centimeters

22. 1 cubic meter = ■ cubic centimeters

23. 6 cubic centimeters = ■ cubic millimeters

24. For the compost boxes in Problem 5.2, find the ratios in parts (a)–(c).

   **a.** the length of each side of the 1-2-3 box to the length of the corresponding side of the 2-4-6 box

   **b.** the surface area of the 1-2-3 box to the surface area of the 2-4-6 box

   **c.** the volume of the 1-2-3 box to the volume of the 2-4-6 box

   **d.** How is each ratio in parts (a)–(c) related to the scale factor from the 1-2-3 box to the 2-4-6 box?

25. At the movie theater, a large cylindrical container of popcorn costs $5.00, and a small cylindrical container costs $2.50. Denzel thinks that the heights of the containers are about the same and that the radius of the large container is about twice the radius of the small container. To get the most popcorn for his $5.00, should Denzel buy one large popcorn or two small popcorns? Explain.

$2.50

$2.50

$5.00

**26.** A compost company builds and sells 1-2-3 compost boxes. They need to store a supply of the boxes in their warehouse to fill customers' orders. The sketches below show a 1-2-3 box on the right and the space in the warehouse allotted for the boxes on the left.

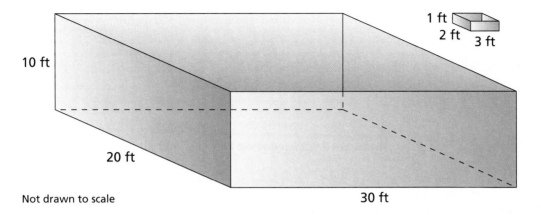

Not drawn to scale

a. How many 1-2-3 boxes can be stored in one layer on the floor of the storage space?

b. How many layers of boxes can be stacked in the storage space?

c. How many boxes can be stored in the storage space?

**27.** Mary's class decides to build a cylindrical compost box. Mary calculates that a cylindrical container with a height of 2 feet and a radius of 1 foot would decompose 0.5 pound of garbage each day. She calls this container a 1-2 cylinder.

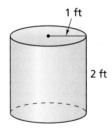

a. How does the volume of the 1-2 cylinder compare with the volume of the 1-2-3 box?

b. How does the surface area of the 1-2 cylinder compare with the surface area of the 1-2-3 box?

c. Mary's class estimates that they throw away about 1 pound of garbage at school each day. What size cylinder should they build to handle this much garbage?

**28.** The two legs of a right triangle are in the ratio 3 : 4.

a. Sketch and label the described triangle. Then sketch and label two other similar right triangles.

b. Suppose you create a similar right triangle by doubling the length of the legs. How will the area of the first triangle be related to the area of the second triangle?

**29.** A football field is 120 yards long, including the end zones, and $53\frac{1}{3}$ yards wide.

  **a.** How many square yards are in the football field?

  **b.** How many square feet are in the football field?

  **c.** What is the relationship between the number of square yards and square feet in the football field?

  **d.** Describe what happens to the number of square feet in the area of a rectangle when the unit of measure for length and width is $\frac{1}{3}$ the size of the original unit.

**For Exercises 30–32, find the volume and surface area of each box shown.**

**30.**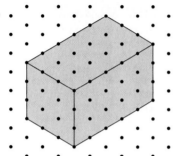

**31.**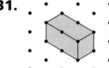

**32.**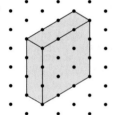

**33.** After a container of water is poured into a cylindrical tank, the tank is $\frac{2}{9}$ full. How many containers of water are needed to fill the tank to $\frac{3}{4}$ full?

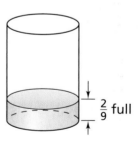

**34.** Anna uses exactly one small can of red paint to cover a strip around the top of an open chest. The red strip around the top is 0.15 of the total surface area (without the top and bottom of the chest).

**a.** How many small cans of blue paint does she need to paint the rest?

**b.** What is the surface area of the chest, not including the top and bottom?

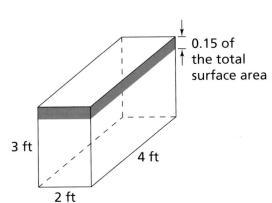

## Extensions

**35.** The following sketches show the front, top, and right side views of a "tilted box" in which two of the six faces are non-rectangular parallelograms. The top and the bottom faces are identical rectangles, and the right and left faces are identical rectangles. (This is called an *oblique prism*.)

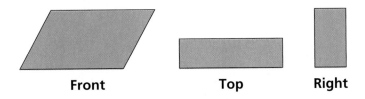

Front        Top        Right

**a.** Make a sketch of the box.

**b.** What measurements do you need to find the volume of the box? How can you use these measurements to find the volume?

**c.** What measurements do you need to find the surface area of the box? How can you use these measurements to find the surface area?

**36.** Is the price of a box of cereal directly related to its volume? Collect some data to help you answer this question.

   **a.** Record the dimensions and prices of two or three different-sized boxes of the same cereal brand.

   **b.** Calculate the volume of each box.

   **c.** Calculate the cost per unit of volume for each box. Compare the results for the different boxes.

   **d.** Write a short report summarizing what you learned about the relationship between box size and cereal price.

**37.** A cake, a loaf of bread, or a brick of cheese could be called a "sliceable" rectangular prism.

   **a.** How many different ways can you slice such a prism into two pieces of equal volume?

   **b.** If the prism were a cube, how many ways could you slice it into two pieces of equal volume?

**For each pair of cylinders in Exercises 38–40, find the ratio of each measurement of Cylinder A to the corresponding measurement of Cylinder B.**

   **a.** the radius          **b.** the height

   **c.** the surface area     **d.** the volume

**38.** The dimensions of Cylinder A are twice the dimensions of Cylinder B.

**39.** The dimensions of Cylinder A are three times the dimensions of Cylinder B.

**40.** The dimensions of Cylinder A are four times the dimensions of Cylinder B.

# Mathematical Reflections 5

**I**n this investigation, you learned how changing the dimensions of a rectangular box affects its volume and surface area. These questions will help you summarize what you have learned.

Think about your answers to these questions. Discuss your ideas with other students and your teacher. Then write a summary of your findings in your notebook.

1. Suppose you want to build a rectangular box with eight times the volume of a given rectangular box. How can you determine the possible dimensions for the new box? Are the two boxes similar? Explain.

2. Describe how the volume and surface area of a rectangular prism change as each of its dimensions is doubled, tripled, quadrupled, and so on.

# Unit Project

## The Package Design Contest

The Worldwide Sporting Company (WSC) wants a new set of package designs for their table-tennis balls (Ping-Pong balls). The table-tennis balls are about 3.8 centimeters in diameter. WSC has decided to offer a scholarship to the students or groups of students who convince the company to use their design.

- The board of directors wants a small package, a medium package, and a large package of table-tennis balls.

- The president of the company wants the cost of the packages to be considered.

- The marketing division wants the packages to be appealing to customers, to stack easily, and to look good on store shelves.

### Part 1: Design a Contest Entry

You are to prepare an entry for the package design contest. Your task is to design three different packages for table-tennis balls. Include the following things in your contest entry:

1. A description of the shape or shapes of the packages you have designed and an explanation for why you selected these shapes.

2. Nets for each of your packages that, when they are cut out, folded, and taped together, will make models of your packages. Use centimeter grid paper to make your patterns.

3. Calculations of how much each of your package designs will cost to construct. The packaging material costs $0.005 per square centimeter.

## Part 2: Write a Report

You will submit your designs and a written proposal to WSC. Your written proposal should try to convince WSC that your designs are the ones they should use.

**4.** An explanation of how you have addressed WSC's three concerns (listed above).

Remember, you are trying to persuade WSC that your designs are the best and that they should select your work. Your report is to be written to the company officials. You need to think about the presentation of your written proposal. It should be neat (maybe even typed!), well organized, and easy to read so that the company officials can follow your work and ideas easily.

# Looking Back and Looking Ahead

## Unit Review

**Go Online**
PHSchool.com

**For:** Vocabulary Review
Puzzle
**Web Code:** anj-6051

**W**hile working on the problems in this unit, you developed strategies for finding *surface area*, *volume*, and *nets* for rectangular prisms and cylinders. You used the relationships of other figures to cylinders to find the volumes of shapes such as *cones, spheres,* and *square pyramids*. Finally, you discovered the effects of enlargement and reduction on dimensions, surface area, and volume of prisms.

## Use Your Understanding: Volume and Surface Area

To test your understanding of volume and surface area, consider the following problems.

**1.** Below is a net for a rectangular prism.

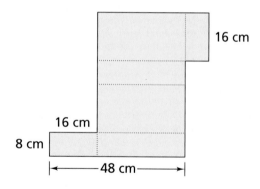

16 cm

16 cm

8 cm

48 cm

   **a.** What are the dimensions of the box that can be made from the net?

   **b.** What is the surface area of the box?

   **c.** What is the volume of the box?

   **d.** Draw two other nets that will produce boxes of the same size and shape.

**2.** Sweet-Smile Chocolates is marketing a special assortment of caramels. The company wants to put the 40 individual caramels into a rectangular box. Each caramel is a 1-inch cube. The caramels should completely fill the box.

**a.** Which arrangement of caramels requires the most cardboard for a box?

**b.** Which arrangement of caramels requires the least cardboard?

**c.** Make sketches of the boxes you described in parts (a) and (b). Label the dimensions.

**d.** Suppose each dimension of the box in part (b) is doubled. How many more caramels can be packaged in the new box?

**3.** The Just-Add-Water Company has decided to change the packaging for a juuice drink. The drink used to come in cylindrical containers with a base diameter of 6 inches and a height of 10 inches. The new container is a square prism that fits inside the old cylinder, as shown in the sketch.

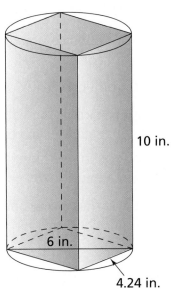

10 in.

6 in.

4.24 in.

**a.** What is the volume of the original cylindrical container?

**b.** How much less juice can the rectangular prism hold than the cylindrical container?

**c.** Suppose that the cost per cubic inch of juice is to be the same for both containers. The original container of juice cost $2.19. How much should a new box of juice cost if the amount of juice per dollar is the same?

**d.** The company is also considering selling the juice in a cone with the same volume as the cylinder. Describe the possible dimensions for such a cone.

## Explain Your Reasoning

**To answer problems about surface area and volume of solid figures, you have to know the meaning of those terms and some strategies for calculating the measurements from given dimensions of various figures.**

**4.** What do *volume* and *surface area* measurements tell about a solid figure?

**5.** Which formulas will show how to find the surface area *A* and the volume *V* of each figure?

    **a.** a rectangular prism

    **b.** a cylinder

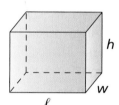

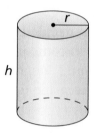

**6.** How can you convince someone that the formulas given in Exercise 5 are correct?

**7.** How are the volumes of cylinders, cones, and spheres related?

**8. a.** Suppose you know the volume of an object such as a box, a cylinder, or a cone. Can you determine its surface area?

    **b.** Suppose you know the surface area of an object. Can you find the volume?

**9.** How are the surface areas and volumes of square pyramids related to cubes?

## Look Ahead

Measurement of surface area and volume for solid figures is used in many practical, scientific, and engineering problems. You will encounter the key ideas about area and volume in future *Connected Mathematics* units, in other mathematics subjects such as geometry, and in many situations of daily life such as packing, storing, and building tasks.

**B**

**base** The face of a three-dimensional shape chosen to be the "bottom" face.

**base** La cara de una figura tridimensional elegida para que sea la cara de la "base."

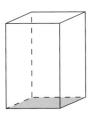 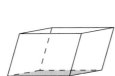   

**C**

**cone** A three-dimensional shape with a circular base and a vertex opposite the base.

**cono** Figura tridimensional con una base circular y un vértice opuesto a la base.

**cube** A three-dimensional shape with six identical square faces.

**cubo** Una figura tridimensional con seis caras cuadradas idénticas.

**cylinder** A three-dimensional shape with two opposite faces that are congruent circles. The side (lateral surface) is a rectangle that is "wrapped around" the circular faces at the ends.

**cilindro** Una figura tridimensional con dos caras opuestas que son círculos congruentes. El lado (la cara lateral) rectángulo es un está "envuelto alrededor de" que las dos caras circulares es los extremos.

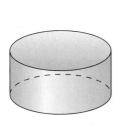 

**edge** A line segment formed where two faces of a three-dimensional shape meet.

**arista** El segmento de recta formado donde se encuentran dos caras de una figura tridimensional.

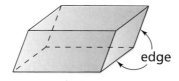

**face** A flat two-dimensional surface of a three-dimensional shape.

**cara** Superficie plana, bidimensional de una figura tridimensional.

**height** The vertical distance between the face chosen to be the base and

- the opposite face of a prism or cylinder, or
- the vertex of a cone or pyramid.

**altura** La distencia vertical entre la cara elegida para ser base y

- la cara opuesta de un prisma o cilindro, o
- el vértice de un cono o pirámide.

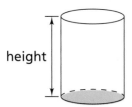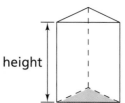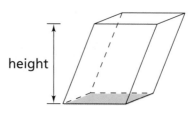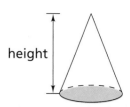

**net** A two-dimensional pattern that can be folded into a three-dimensional figure.

**patrón plano** Un patrón bidimensional que se puede plegar para formar una figura tridimensional.

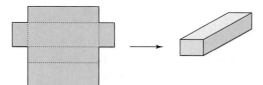

**oblique prism**  A prism whose side faces are non-rectangular parallelograms.

**prisma oblicuo**  Prisma cuyas caras laterales son paralelogramos no rectangulares.

**prism**  A three-dimensional shape with a top and bottom (base) that are congruent polygons and lateral faces that are parallelograms.

**prisma**  Una figura tridimensional cuya parte superior y cuyo fondo (base) son polígonos congruentes y cuyas caras laterales son paralelogramos.

**pyramid**  A three-dimensional shape with one polygonal base and lateral sides that are all triangles that meet at a vertex opposite the base.

**pirámide**  Figura tridimensional cuya base es un polígono y cuyas caras laterales son tríangulos que se encuentran en un vértice opuesto a la base.

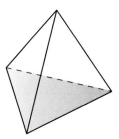
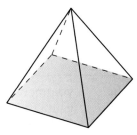
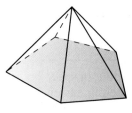

**rectangular prism**  A prism with a top and bottom (base) that are congruent rectangles.

**prisma rectangular**  Un prisma cuya parte superior e inferior (base) son rectángulos congruentes.

**Right rectangular prism**

**Oblique rectangular prism**

English/Spanish Glossary

**right prism** A prism whose vertical faces are rectangles. The bases are congruent polygons.

**prisma recto** Un prisma cuyas caras verticales son rectángulos. Los bases son polígonos congruentes.

**S**

**sphere** A three-dimensional shape whose surface consists of all the points that are a given distance from the center of the shape.

**esfera** Una figura tridimensional cuya superficie consiste en todos los puntos ubicados a una distancia dada del centro de la figura.

**surface area** The area required to cover a three-dimensional shape.

**área total** El área requerida para cubrir una figura tridimensional.

**U**

**unit cube** A cube whose edges are 1 unit long. It is the basic unit of measurement for volume.

**unidad cúbica** Un cubo cuyas aristas miden 1 unidad de longitud. Es la unidad básica de medición para el volumen.

**V**

**volume** The amount of space occupied by, or the capacity of, a three-dimensional shape. The volume is the number of unit cubes that will fit into a three-dimensional shape.

**volumen** La cantidad de espacio que ocupa una figura tridimensional o la capacidad de dicha figura. Es el número de unidades cúbicas que cabrán en una figura tridimensional.

# Index

# Acknowledgments

## Team Credits

The people who made up the **Connected Mathematics 2** team—representing editorial, editorial services, design services, and production services—are listed below. Bold type denotes core team members.

Leora Adler, Judith Buice, Kerry Cashman, Patrick Culleton, Sheila DeFazio, Richard Heater, **Barbara Hollingdale, Jayne Holman,** Karen Holtzman, **Etta Jacobs,** Christine Lee, Carolyn Lock, Catherine Maglio, **Dotti Marshall,** Rich McMahon, Eve Melnechuk, Kristin Mingrone, Terri Mitchell, **Marsha Novak,** Irene Rubin, Donna Russo, Robin Samper, Siri Schwartzman, **Nancy Smith,** Emily Soltanoff, **Mark Tricca,** Paula Vergith, Roberta Warshaw, Helen Young

## Additional Credits

Diana Bonfilio, Mairead Reddin, Michael Torocsik, nSight, Inc.

## Technical Illustration

WestWords, Inc.

## Cover Design

tom white.images

## Photos

**2,** Getty Images, Inc.; **3,** Geri Engberg; **5,** Jeff Greenberg/PhotoEdit; **9,** Jack Kurt/The Image Works; **15,** photolibrary.com pty. ltd./Index Stock Imagery, Inc.; **16,** Digital Vision/Getty Images, Inc.; **20,** Laura Dwight/PhotoEdit; **27,** BananaStock/Robertstock; **28,** IFA/PictureQuest; **29,** Andrew Olney/Masterfile; **30,** Bob Daemmrich/PhotoEdit; **37,** Lynn Stone/Getty Images, Inc.; **39,** Danita Delimont/Alamy; **40,** Richard Haynes; **42,** Getty Images, Inc.; **45,** Sam Yeh/AFP/Getty Images, Inc.; **52,** Francis Dean/The Image Works; **53,** ©2002 Thaves. Reprinted with permission. Newspaper dist. by NEA, Inc.; **59 l,** Bryan & Cherry Alexander/Photo Researchers, Inc.; **59 r,** A. Woolfitt/Robert Harding World Imagery; **60,** Richard Haynes; **62,** David Young-Wolff/PhotoEdit; **62 inset,** Wally Eberhart/Getty Images, Inc.; **65,** Clayton Sharrard/PhotoEdit; **66,** SuperStock, Inc./SuperStock; **68,** Jeff Mermelstein/Getty Images, Inc.; **69,** Masterfile (Royalty-Free Division); **73,** Richard Haynes; **77,** Brooke Slezak/Getty Images, Inc.